TABLE OF CONTENTS

Page

ACRONYMS

AAR	After Action Report
ACR	Armored Cavalry Regiment
AO	Area of Operations
AQIZ	Al Qaeda in Iraq
ARVN	Army of the Republic of Vietnam (South Vietnam)
BCT	Brigade Combat Team
BCTP	Battle Command Training Program
BN	Battalion
BSP	Baghdad Security Plan
CF	Coalition Forces
C-H-B	Clear-Hold-Build
COG	Center of Gravity
COL	Colonel
COIN	Counterinsurgency
CPA	Coalition Provisional Authority
DoD	Department of Defense
DoS	Department of State
FID	Foreign Internal Defense
FM	Field Manual
FSO	Full Spectrum Operations
GEN	General
GOI	Government of Iraq
GWOT	Global War on Terror (synonymous with War on Terror and Long War)

HBCT	Heavy Brigade Combat Team
HN	Host Nation
IN	Infantry
IZ	DoD country code for Iraq
JAM	Jaysh al Mahdi
LIC	Low Intensity Conflict
LLOs	Logical Lines of Operation
LOE	Lines of Effort
LTC	Lieutenant Colonel
LTG	Lieutenant General
MG	Major General
MNC-I	Operational Headquarters, Multi-National Corps--Iraq
MND-B	Multi-National Division--Baghdad
MNF-I	Strategic Headquarters, Multi-National Force--Iraq
OE	Operating Environment
OIF	Operation Iraqi Freedom
SBCT	Stryker Brigade Combat Team
SECDEF	Secretary of Defense
SECSTATE	Secretary of State
U.S.	United States

ILLUSTRATIONS

CHAPTER 1

INTRODUCTION

Purpose

The purpose of this thesis is to present a tactical design model for

counterinsurgency (COIN) operations for use at the battalion level. This work was

inspired by events and lessons from Baghdad, Iraq throughout 2007 and early 2008. It

addresses the challenges that United States (U.S.) Army tactical formations faced in the

development of effective COIN operations. While the Army's contemporary doctrine on

COIN is highly regarded, it is largely conceptual and offers little practicable utility for

tactical units tasked to execute such operations. This work is meant to address this

shortcoming by presenting a suitable design tool for tactical formations to reference while

developing COIN operations.

Background

Seated before a congressional delegation comprised of members of the Senate

Foreign Relations Committee in October 2005, Secretary of State (SECSTATE)

Condoleezza Rice began to outline the emergent strategy that would shift the U.S.

Government's approach in Iraq.[1] This strategy transformed the parallel diplomatic and

military efforts of the U.S. into a convergent, unified approach designed to address the

rapidly deteriorating situation in Iraq. Operation Iraqi Freedom (OIF) was approaching

the end of its third year and Secretary Rice's testimony had just offered the State

Department's newest policy concerning its role in the COIN. This testimony came to be

the at-large strategic, operational, and tactical approach towards stabilizing the turbulent

1

country. Secretary Rice's three-pronged strategy of "clearing the toughest places . . . working to hold and steadily enlarge these secure areas . . . working to build truly national institutions,"[2] would shortly become the multi-level operational design model in OIF: Clear, Hold, and Build (C-H-B).

The C-H-B methodology offered a fresh approach to combating the insurgency. President George W. Bush latched onto Secretary Rice's idea and in early 2006 "C-H-B" became the guiding principle for diplomatic and military efforts to combat the insurgency in Iraq. The application of this newly minted approach occurred at the start of 2007. An influx of over 30,000 uniformed service members "surged" to reestablish security in the two most volatile regions of Iraq: the nation's largest city and capital, Baghdad, and the restive Anbar Province. The resulting operation, named the Baghdad Security Plan (BSP), was designed to implement the C-H-B approach. The design of the BSP broke from prior methods of COIN utilized by the Army during OIF. Lower-echelon tactical units were empowered with tremendous autonomy and were relied upon as the prime units of employment. Despite the perception that "the surge" facilitated nothing but a large scale sweep operation, it really amounted to simply a means to establish the resources needed to execute C-H-B operations throughout the capital city.

The BSP was born from an essay contest sponsored by the Combined Arms Center in mid-2006.[3] The cornerstone of the plan was the utilization of the battalion echelon as the primary unit of employment for COIN operations in Baghdad. A battalion's structure, augmented staff, subordinate maneuver units, and especially its ability to remain in close proximity to the population rendered the battalion perfectly suited to conduct COIN operations. While higher tactical echelons were instrumental in

2

coordinating resources and aligning efforts, maneuver battalions would carry the weight of tactical execution.

> This basic unit is the maneuver battalion. Brigades, divisions, and other higher headquarters must establish objectives, coordinate actions, apportion terrain, and allocate national resources among subordinate units. These higher commands are responsible for establishing the channels and means that allow locally embedded maneuver battalions to engage in decisive, practical problem-solving.[4]

The BSP was initiated in February of 2007. Its core design aligned U.S. Army maneuver battalions and Iraqi security elements within compartmented areas throughout Baghdad. These "partnered" military and indigenous security forces were the executors of the C-H-B operations outlined in the plan. Each battalion area of operations was its own microcosm: culture, religious sect, physical terrain, and insurgent dynamics differed vastly from one area to neighboring ones. The notion of establishing the battalion as the preeminent echelon for COIN operations had been realized. Combat battalions quickly discovered that the process of designing and arranging these clearing, holding, and building operations was military art, with little relevant doctrinal "science" to support them.

The Army, at this point, had captured three years of experiences in OIF and was revising its antiquated COIN doctrine. Lieutenant General (LTG) David Petraeus, Commander of the U.S. Army Combined Arms Center from October 2005 to early February 2007, led the effort to develop the COIN FM; a subject matter which the Army had not formally addressed in two decades (with the exception of a stopgap manual for COIN which the Army published in 2004, Field Manual Interim (FMI) 3-07.22, *Counterinsurgency Operations*). The efforts of Petraeus' doctrine team resulted in the U.S. Army's first independent counterinsurgency field manual ever: FM 3-24,

Counterinsurgency, officially published in December of 2006. In addition to serving as the Army's principal guide for COIN, the manual was co-signed by the United States Marine Corps. This signified an important indication of unity since both service components were the primary organizations prosecuting the counterinsurgency in Iraq.

FM 3-24 addresses the CHB approach as one of three viable methods to conduct COIN operations.[5] The level of detail concerning the design of such operations is mostly theoretical however, with little specific material to aid tactical units in the development of COIN operations. FM 3-24.2, *Tactics in Counterinsurgency* (in draft form at the time of this paper's publication), somewhat addresses the principles for designing C-H-B operations, though still not to any significant degree. For instance, the draft offers no model for tactical echelons to utilize as a framework for designing COIN operations.[6] As a result, this void in doctrine concerning how to tactically design C-H-B operations at battalion-level created many challenges during the execution of the BSP. The following research is structured to address this void and to derive a model for tactical units to design more effective Clear-Hold-Build operations.

<u>Primary Research Question</u>

What is a suitable tactical design model for the development of battalion-level COIN operations utilizing the C-H-B approach?

<u>Secondary Research Questions</u>

<u>Secondary Question 1</u>: Is the doctrinal guidance concerning C-H-B operations relevant and adequate to guide a battalion in designing such operations? If not, what is missing or in need of revision?

<u>Secondary Question 2</u>: What are the common themes shared by battalions when designing successful C-H-B operations? What are the common points of failure?

<u>Secondary Question 3</u>: Do the elements of operational design found in FM 3-0, *Operations*, provide an adequate framework for battalions to design and plan C-H-B operations successfully? If not, what is a viable structure for designing operations at the battalion level?

<u>Chapter Outline</u>

The chapters that follow provide the background and analysis to help determine the answers to these research questions. This thesis aims to give the reader a broader sense of the historical roots of the C-H-B approach to COIN and why it is so inherently critical for tactical formations to understand the theory involved in designing such operations.

Chapter 2 outlines the materials utilized as primary and secondary sources throughout this thesis. These resources range from doctrinal materials to contemporary reports pertaining to COIN operations executed during Operation Iraqi Freedom. The paper is balanced with several historical vignettes that present the roots of the Army's current COIN paradigms.

The third chapter involves two historical case studies of Army COIN operations and identifies the underpinnings of today's C-H-B approach. The first case study provides a broad analysis of the Army's counterinsurgency culture of the Vietnam era. This study concludes that the U.S. Army did not have the requisite understanding, doctrine, or commitment to execute COIN operations in Vietnam. It also concludes that the Army's experiences in Southeast Asia did very little to shape the force during the interim period from 1975 to the start of the Global War on Terror in 2001.

The second historical case study details actions by the 3rd Armored Cavalry Regiment (ACR) in the Iraqi city of Tal Afar from 2005 to 2006. This study segues into recent history and presents the genesis of the C-H-B approach as it is known today. Tal Afar, a major focal point of operations in 2005, was wracked by insurgent-fomented violence. Secretary Rice cited the successful COIN campaign conducted by 3rd ACR as she presented the broader concepts of clearing, holding, and building during her testimony to Congress in October of 2005. Her testimony, presented earlier in this chapter, was the formal introduction of the concept of C-H-B to the public, and set the stage for its eventual adoption by the Army and Marine Corps as a doctrinal principle. The 3rd ACR case study illustrates the tactical design of successful counterinsurgency operations against the Sunni insurgent movement that plagued Tal Afar and impacted the operational and strategic environments of Iraq. The tactical design utilized by 3rd ACR demonstrated the importance of empowering the lowest echelons of command to conduct protracted COIN operations.

Analysis of the COIN lessons of Vietnam and Tal Afar provides the historical context for understanding how the U.S. Army evolved its methodology by early 2007. This thesis finds quite significant that no notable Army or Marine Corps doctrinal advancements specific to COIN warfare occurred from 1975 to 2005.

Chapter 4 considers this surprising fact and weighs it against short case studies involving C-H-B operations executed during the BSP. These case studies detail how two battalion-sized task forces tactically designed COIN operations. The studies depict how

6

these units interpreted COIN doctrine presented in FM 3-24 to meet the design requirements of battalion operations in Baghdad. These two studies facilitate the establishment of a tactical design model for COIN operations. The design model offers tactical echelons (particularly battalion and task-force sized organizations) a suitable framework for establishing C-H-B operations.

Chapter 5 uses the analysis from Chapters 3 and 4 and synthesizes it with current Army doctrine to fashion a perspective on how tactical units can suitably design COIN operations. The elements of operational design, found in chapter six of FM 3-0, *Operations*, serve as the basis for this synthesis.

Chapter 6 summarizes the conclusions and recommendations drawn from the research. The principal conclusion, or product of this thesis, is a tactical design model for COIN operations. This model represents an integration of the elements of operational design with current COIN doctrine, and provides a tool for tactical echelons to use in the development of COIN operations.

Significance of Research

This topic of study is critical to the success of U.S. Forces in one of America's longest and costliest wars, because counterinsurgencies are largely fought at the tactical level. The potential for battalion-centric C-H-B operations to continue, both in Iraq and Afghanistan as well as future theaters, is very high. This research questions whether COIN doctrine, published in the December 2006 release of FM 3-24, *Counterinsurgency*, and drafted in FM 3-24.2, *Tactics in Counterinsurgency*, adequately addresses the design and execution of Clear-Hold-Build operations at the battalion level. Since COIN operations appear to be a key element of the U.S. Army's "Persistent Conflict" perspective, this research could prove valuable for improving combat battalions' ability to tactically design protracted COIN operations.

Assumptions

Future conflicts in the War on Terror will involve COIN and will present similar conditions to those currently existing in Iraq. These conflicts will warrant the commitment of U.S. Army combat formations with battalions serving as the preeminent unit for execution of Clear-Hold-Build COIN operations.

The doctrinal base for executing COIN operations will not soon change from the published doctrine found in FM 3-24 dated December 2006 and from broader operational guidance found in FM 3-0, *Operations*, dated February 2008. However, this doctrinal base will become enriched through its application to current conflicts in Iraq and Afghanistan.

Battalions will continue to train for and operate within protracted COIN environments. Senior commanders in such environments will expect battalions to synchronize their efforts with the doctrinal approach of C-H-B operations and the tenets of COIN found in FM 3-24 and its supporting manuals still in development (such as FM 3-24.2, *Tactics in Counterinsurgency*).

The basic conditions that define a counterinsurgent environment will be replicated in geographical areas to which the United States commits military forces in the future.

Limitations

The youth of the C-H-B concept limits the availability of documented application to U.S. experiences in OIF. Many of the sources that have guided this study are scholarly works, essays, and research papers that have emerged over the past several years and have not benefited from historical reflection or perspective.

The application of the C-H-B approach has implications from the strategic level of war down to the tactical level. For the sake of maintaining a workable scope, the thesis remains solely oriented to the tactical level of warfare with a focus on the battalion level of organization and command.

This thesis focuses on the conduct of COIN operations in Iraq. The resulting recommendations are general enough to support COIN operations in other contexts.

The conclusions and recommendations presented in Chapter 6 are most relevant to operating environments that have matured into protracted counterinsurgency campaigns. Today's spectrum of conflict requires a broad range of application of military force. COIN environments may entail different levels of commitment of military resources. This study outlines a method for designing C-H-B COIN operations for conventional Army tactical maneuver formations. The model will not work for Limited Support or Combined Action campaigns.[7]

This study may not be adaptable to all theaters of operation. It is intended, however, to derive a universal framework for designing tactical COIN operations utilizing the C-H-B approach. The design principles offered in the final chapters may not be practicable in certain conditions since geographic, religious, cultural, and political dynamics may differ greatly from one insurgent environment to the next.

Since COIN is born from an opponent's political agenda, it is difficult to dismiss the hypothetical political framework, which drives such operations. The work involved in this thesis does not overtly analyze political and diplomatic motives, nor do these factors

9

bear much weight in the findings and conclusions. Since the focus of the study rests at lower tactical levels, it was important to consider political agendas but not treat them extensively.

Finally, FM 3-24.2, *Tactics in Counterinsurgency*, existed in draft form during the creation of this document. The November 2008 draft contains sections detailing tactical design and planning of COIN operations. This paper largely considered the materials found in this draft of FM 3-24.2 since they are highly relevant. This writer quickly discovered that the draft *Tactics in Counterinsurgency* suffers from the same crucial shortcoming as FM 3-24: neither manual offers lower tactical formations a suitable model for design of C-H-B COIN operations.

Delimitations

This thesis deals with the holistic analysis of historical lessons, current doctrine, and recent U.S. Army experiences in COIN environments. It is not affected by a lack of established and time-tested resources that address the contemporary implementation of modern COIN approaches and strategies.

The design of this paper addresses current U.S. Army doctrine and theory, including potential shortfalls in tactical level planning methodologies. While FM 3-24 also serves as the U.S. Marine Corps' manual on COIN, the conclusions were derived from the study of the U.S. Army's perspective on COIN operations. The results may be adequate for other service elements, but the intent was to build a construct which U.S. Army battalions could adopt to help shape the design of C-H-B operations.

The nature of modern COIN operations has seemingly dulled the lines between operational and tactical planning and design considerations. Additionally, the organization and capabilities of modern U.S. Army Brigade Combat Teams (BCTs) have

dramatically been increased through the process of force transformation. A BCT and its

subordinate maneuver units now benefit from larger, more capable staffs and control

critical combat enablers. Often these units have some degree of joint service

representation. Therefore, the line between operational and tactical inputs into a

campaign plan has been further reduced. The formulation of an operational campaign

plan focusing on COIN efforts is largely driven by tactical considerations. It is arguable

that campaign planning for a COIN environment may have greater utility at the tactical

level. The military term "campaign" is defined by FM 3-0 as the following:

> A *campaign* is a series of related major operations aimed at achieving strategic
> and operational objectives within a given time and space (JP 5-0). Campaigns are
> always joint operations. Campaigns exploit the advantages of interdependent
> Service capabilities through unified action. Coordinated, synchronized, and
> integrated action is necessary to reestablish civil authority after joint operations
> end, even when combat is not required. Effective joint and Army operations
> require all echelons to perform extensive collaborative planning and understand
> joint interdependence.[8]

The idea that the spirit of a campaign resides at only the operational and strategic

levels of warfare needs to be examined critically. The nature of fighting an insurgency

mandates the need to empower lower echelons to achieve operational and strategic effects

through tactically protracted commitment. This argument is strengthened by the fact that

battalions operating in Iraq today typically have joint service representation and interact

frequently with other governmental and supporting agencies. Additionally, the dynamics

of an insurgency often vastly differ from one neighborhood to the next. These two

factors, coupled with the idea that tactical C-H-B operations themselves often times

directly contribute to higher-order objectives, convince this writer that tactical units are

capable of executing operations within a campaign-quality COIN framework. The nondoctrinal term "tactical campaign," is periodically utilized to capture the essence of this dynamic.

Research Design

The research design utilized in this study is a modified qualitative case study organized through analysis of key historical events and the study of the application of doctrine. This research fuses recent events from operations during execution of the BSP with case studies from Vietnam and OIF prior to 2007. The historical case studies found in Chapter 3 offer several perspectives of the U.S. Army's involvement in COIN operations from the Vietnam era through the early years of OIF. Chapter 4 utilizes these historical vignettes to analyze a study of two battalion-sized organizations that participated in the BSP. The research relies upon historical and doctrinal qualitative analysis to guide all judgments. Chapter 5 offers the synthesis of this qualitative analysis and establishes the basis for the findings presented in the final chapter. Chapter 6 presents the conclusions and recommendations developed through this research process.

Chapter Conclusion

Chapter 1 has outlined the purpose and construct of the thesis. It described the research questions and parameters by which these questions are researched, considered, analyzed, and presented. Chapter 2 details the materials and resources that aided the development of this thesis.

_____

[1]U.S. Department of State, Secretary of State's Remarks, http://www.state.gov/ secretary/rm/2005/55303.htm (accessed 23 September 2008.

[2]Ibid.

[3]Douglas A.Ollivant and Eric D. Chewning, "Producing Victory: Rethinking Conventional Forces in Counterinsurgency Operations," *Military Review* (July-August 2006): 50-59.

[4]Ibid., 56.

[5]Department of the Army, Field Manual (FM) 3-24, *Counterinsurgency* (Washington, DC: Government Printing Office, 2006), 5-18 through 5-25.

[6]Department of the Army, Field Manual (FM) 3-24.2 (Draft), *Tactics in Counterinsurgency* (Washington, DC: Government Printing Office, 2008), 4-1 through 4-12.

[7]Department of the Army, FM 3-24, 5-23 through 5-25.

[8]Department of the Army, Field Manual (FM) 3-0, *Operations* (Washington, DC: Government Printing Office, 2008), 1-10.

CHAPTER 2

COUNTERINSURGENCY LITERATURE REVIEW

Research Material Overview

Literature regarding contemporary U.S. approaches to counterinsurgency is growing exponentially. Despite being a recent topic of concern, many worthwhile pieces have been written over the past five years. While most of these resources do not specifically detail the Army's application of the C-H-B approach, a number deal with its theory or methodology. The most pronounced limitation of this research stems from the scarcity of declassified material pertaining to U.S. Army C-H-B operations executed during the BSP in 2007 to 2008.

Periodicals, professional blogs covering defense issues, and catalogued interviews with recent veterans have provided some of the background information for this paper. A portion of the resources utilized has come from declassified operational summaries from Iraq. A number of new books from 2008 concerning the planning and execution of the BSP provided beneficial material. The account outlining the operational design and implementation of the BSP by Linda Robinson, *Tell Me How This Ends: General David Petraeus and the Search for a Way Out of Iraq*, was instrumental in detailing the framework that governed the tactics of C-H-B operations.

It is generally the common perception that nothing on today's battlefield, with the exception of the relative technological advances, differs vastly from prior military endeavors. That is certainly the case when analyzing 21st century COIN operations. One cannot make significant distinctions between today's COIN operating environments and those experienced throughout the past century. Classic pieces such as David Galula's

Counterinsurgency Warfare: Theory and Practice as well as Charles Calwell's *Small Wars: Their Principles and Practice* helped to provide a foundation of historical counterinsurgency insight. These works, along with other relative and more contemporary material, such as John A. Nagl's *Counterinsurgency Lessons From Malaya and Vietnam: Learning to Eat Soup with a Knife*, allowed the establishment of adequate historical parallels to our modern doctrine for COIN operations. These resources also helped to determine the ancestry of the Clear-Hold-Build.

The U.S. Army Field Manual 3-24, *Counterinsurgency*, and its parent manual 3-0, Operations, provided an institutional azimuth. An assortment of monographs and other research papers, professional articles, lessons learned compilations, and documented experiences have all been utilized to shape an understanding of how best to establish a tactical design model for COIN operations.

The bibliography found at the conclusion of this thesis attempts to be inclusive. Many of the sources are directly referenced throughout the paper, but many were simply used as supplements to broaden the understanding of COIN theory.

<u>Doctrinal Resources</u>

Failures, particularly in the American involvement in Iraq, have driven systemic, doctrinal, and operational changes throughout the U.S. Army. Three of the Army's most heralded institutional manuals have already benefited from the lessons learned in the Iraqi theater of war from 2003 to 2006. Field Manual 3-0, *Operations*, FM 3-24, *Counterinsurgency*, and Field Manual 3-07, *Stability Operations* were released during the timeframe of December 2006 through October 2008. These documents are designed to establish the conceptual baseline for how operations, including COIN, are managed, led, and fought.

Field Manual 3-0, the principal document outlining the U.S. Army's methods of employment throughout the range of operational environments, delivers the framework for how the Army is to conduct "Full Spectrum Operations."[1] This concept involves the weighted application of offensive, defensive and stability-type operations in order to achieve the integrated strategic, operational, and tactical results in a contingency operation.[2]

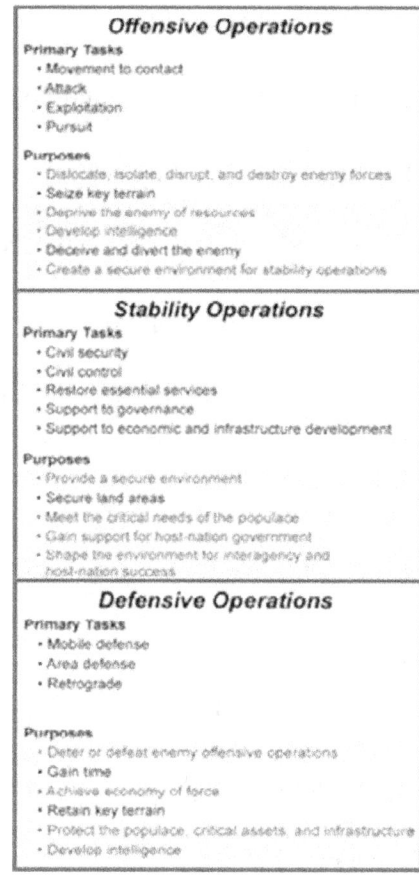

Figure 1.   Major Elements of Full-Spectrum Operations With Purposes
Source: Department of the Army, Field Manual 3-0, *Operations* (Washington, DC: Government Printing Office, 2008), 3-7. (Note: The highlighted purposes are directly linked to COIN operations.)

As outlined in paragraph 3-40 of FM 3-0, COIN operations combine both offensive and stability tasks to achieve decisive results.[3] Subsequent analysis of FM 3-24, *Counterinsurgency*, yields the notion that defensive operations, perhaps in a more nuanced fashion than traditionally thought (such as providing security to protect the local populace and critical infrastructure), are also inherently important to the successful conduct of COIN Operations.

Field Manual 3-0 specifically notes that COIN is the dominant type of operation being conducted in OIF.[4] This fact stresses the relevance of figure 1 by concretely supporting the premise that COIN operations involve application of the entire spectrum of operations, except civil support since such operations are limited to domestic reaches.

FM 3-0 notes, critically for this study, that lower echelon tactical units, especially battalion or task force-sized organizations, are the prime units of employment for COIN operations. This manual indicates that most COIN operations are executed at the squad, platoon, and company levels. However, it is the battalion headquarters that provides effective direction and resource allocation to allow its lower tactical echelons to achieve the desired results.[5]

This statement, that the battalion echelon is the key unit of employment for COIN operations is noteworthy for two reasons. First, this indicates that the U.S. Army has recognized that the COIN operating environment is one of microcosms. This also implies that higher echelon headquarters (brigade and above) cannot effectively visualize tactical COIN problems nor directly execute actions toward accomplishing a military end state in such an environment. This is an important inference, since it places operational and even strategic responsibilities for countering an insurgency at lower tactical levels.

Secondly, this concept supports the theory that the battalion level is the most suitable echelon for execution of COIN operations. In an environment where the lines of separation between strategic, operational, and tactical outcomes are significantly blurred, it is possible to think in terms of "campaigning" when trying to understand how a battalion would approach the challenges of conducting protracted COIN operations.

FM 3-24, *Counterinsurgency*, was the first of the three prominent doctrinal manuals to be released. Published in December of 2006, FM 3-24 was heralded as the most important piece of professional literature that the U.S. Army had fielded in decades. This manual was written to govern how two branches of service (the U.S. Army and U.S. Marine Corps) would conceptually approach a COIN environment. The supervisor of development and the timing of the publication's release were important factors that added to the manual's notoriety. David Petraeus, a LTG and commander of the Combined Arms Center at Fort Leavenworth at the time, provided oversight for the manual's doctrine development team. Two months after this manual's release in February of 2007, LTG Petraeus was promoted to the rank of General and became the Multi-National Force--Iraq (MNF-I) commander, and thus, the theater strategic commander for the war in Iraq. He found himself in the most advantageous position to inject the materials from FM 3-24 as execution of the BSP started on February 14th, 2007--less than one week after he took command of MNF-I.

The COIN manual was the first bona fide doctrinal manual to encapsulate the practice of COIN warfare since the 1986 release of FM 90-8, *Counterguerrilla Operations*. Unlike its predecessor, FM 3-24 is expansive in regards to historical context, theory, and application of general COIN principles. The materials in FM 3-24 apply mostly to the operational level of warfare. It is a field manual of higher order and perspective, and it does not provide much in the way of tactical application of the theory it presents.

Chapter 4 of FM 3-24 gives focus to the importance of sound operational design for successful COIN operations. It defines the purpose of operational design as being "to achieve a greater understanding, a proposed solution based on that understanding, and a means to learn and adapt."[6] This chapter also addresses the complexity in designing COIN operations:

> Design and planning are qualitatively different yet interrelated activities essential for solving complex problems. While planning activities receive consistent emphasis in both doctrine and practice, discussion of design remains largely abstract and is rarely practiced. Presented a problem, staffs often rush directly into planning without clearly understanding the complex environment of the situation, purpose of military involvement, and approach required to address the core issues. This situation is particularly problematic with insurgencies. Campaign design informs and is informed by planning and operations. It has an intellectual foundation that aids continuous assessment of operations and the operational environment. Commanders should lead the design process and communicate the resulting framework to other commanders for planning, preparation, and execution.[7]

The fundamental model of tactical design for a COIN environment is the focal point for this thesis. Chapter 4 of FM 3-24 provides rudimentary guidelines for conceptual application of the "Elements of Operational Design" found in FM 3-0, *Operations*, dated 2008. The elements of operational design are the principles by which a campaign or major operation is established at the operational level of war. The elements, highlighted below in figure 2, help to identify a problem, design a framework to address the problem, and then provide a means to refine the design to fit the actuality of the operating environment.

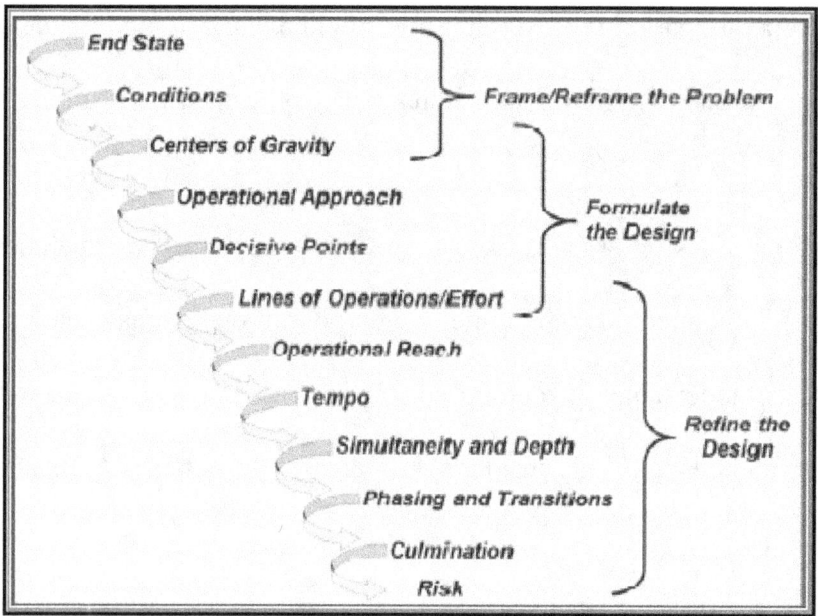

Figure 2.   Elements of Operational Design

Source: Department of the Army, Field Manual 3-0, *Operations* (Washington, DC: Government Printing Office, 2008), 6-7.

The challenge in applying the Elements of Operational Design is that the construct is too general for tactical echelons. Nowhere in FM 3-24, nor in any other doctrinal manual, can you find a tactical design model for COIN-themed operations. Subsequent chapters in this paper analyze the viability and suitability of the elements of operational design at the tactical level within the context of COIN operations.

Chapter 5 of FM 3-24 addresses three approaches utilized for conducting COIN operations. These three approaches are C-H-B, Combined Action, and Limited Support. These approaches are not mutually exclusive, but are utilized at different phases of a strategic COIN campaign to achieve desired effects. Of note, of these three techniques only the C-H-B approach is purely relevant to Title X (Ten) environments--situations that are governed by the Department of Defense and supported by other governmental agencies. The C-H-B approach requires wholesale, protracted commitment of military fighting formations to combat an insurgency. Therefore it is the only approach that warrants a tactical design model.

The C-H-B approach, as defined by FM 3-24, "is executed in a specific, high-priority area experiencing overt insurgent operations"[8] and has the following primary objectives:

1. Create a secure physical and psychological environment.

2. Establish firm government control of the populace and area.

3. Gain the populace's support.[9]

This approach is commonly viewed in terms of the "Three Block War" construct.[10] Clearing elements neutralize insurgent threats and support networks in the first block. This is accomplished through a series of offensive actions, direct engagements, searches, and zone-type clearance missions. The middle block is the area where gains are consolidated and held. It is here that the host nation security forces establish capacity to retain security gains. The last block of the model is where the building takes place. This "building" encompasses both physical and logical manifestations focused on maintaining security of the populace, infrastructure, and governmental integrity and sovereignty. Examples of physical building operations include establishing blast walls, outposts, and police checkpoints. Logical building involves developing rapport with local leadership, introducing the rule of law, legitimizing authority, and earning the trust and support of the populace. The trust, support, and security of the populace represent the decisive point which operations in the "build" category hope to achieve. Therefore, the final block (despite the U.S. Army's seeming predisposition to focus on the lead block), is the true determining factor in successful execution of C-H-B operations. It can accurately be labeled the "building block" of success for a counterinsurgency.

While the material found in FM 3-24 provides rough guidelines for the development of operational or campaign design, it does so in broad terms. Little of the manual can be easily modified for use at the tactical level. A supporting manual to FM 3-24 is being developed to address this shortcoming. Field Manual 3-24.2, *Tactics in Counterinsurgency*, presents tactical COIN theory and application. This manual was in draft form at publication of this paper. There is little material in the draft of FM 3-24.2 that directly addresses tactical COIN design however. Despite having a section devoted to "Tactical Design in Counterinsurgency" the draft fails to offer a framework for designing such operations. Tactical echelons, specifically maneuver battalions, are left to interpret both FM 3-24 and FM 3-24.2 arbitrarily. For this reason, it is the intent of this thesis to fill in this doctrinal void and establish a design methodology for tactical units to utilize for C-H-B operations.

The last major resource in the doctrinal category is David Galula's authoritative compilation of COIN theories and axioms, *Counterinsurgency Warfare: Theory and Practices*. From this writer's perspective, this book is as good as doctrine. Galula's perspectives have lost no relevance over the past 50 years. This is evident by its prominent listing in the FM 3-24 bibliography. Galula himself presented the principles that serve as the theory behind the Clear-Hold-Build approach--considerations that were easy for current doctrine writers to employ.

Galula's ideas of neutralizing adversarial forces, followed by employment of a standing security force and coercion of the populace to prevent reintroduction of insurgent elements[11], are principles on which we have built our revisionist doctrinal base today. His tenets for conducting COIN operations are linked to the modern concept of applying tactical formations against the same types of problems that he faced in North Africa in the mid-20th century. The below extract from a Battle Command Training Program briefing to an HBCT prior to deployment to Iraq contains the modern evolution of Galula's premises found in Chapter 7 of *Counterinsurgency Warfare.*

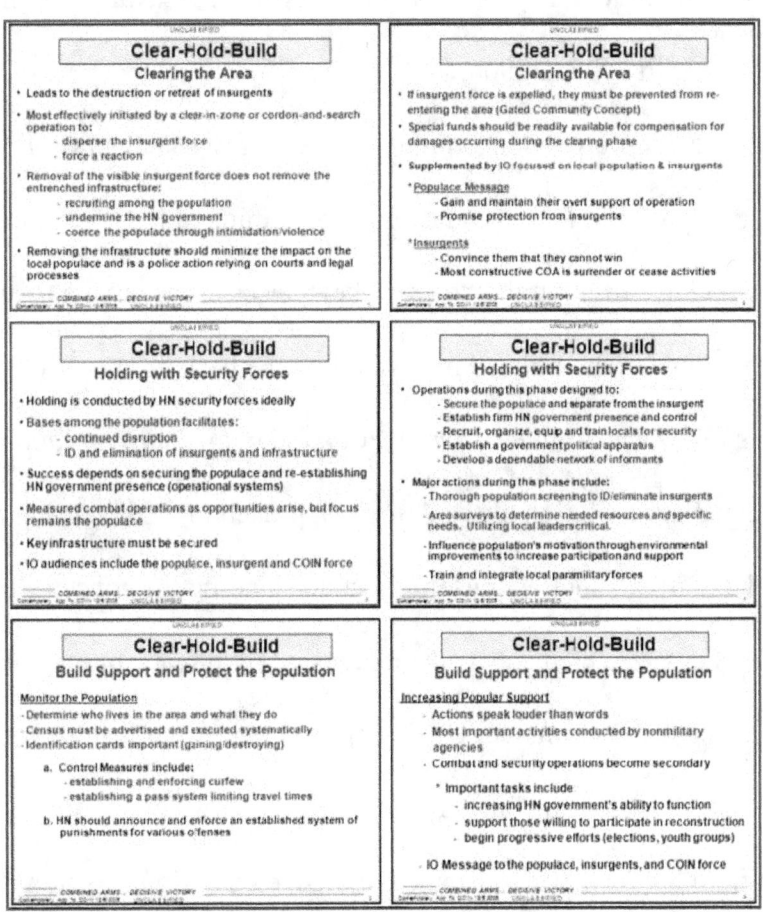

Figure 3.   BCTP Instruction on C-H-B Theory to 4-3 HBCT in January 2007
Source: Battle Command Training Program, Fort Leavenworth, KS, 22 January 2007

Historical Case Study Resources

In order to understand the dynamics of modern COIN operations, it is first necessary to analyze U.S. Army counterinsurgency thinking in recent history. This paper broadly assesses the Army's tactical COIN experiences in Vietnam from 1965 to 1973. While the Army supported several COIN operations from the conclusion of Vietnam to the start of OIF (such as Columbia, El Salvador, Nicaragua, and Somalia), none of these efforts involved the protracted commitment of conventional formations. Therefore, the next historical data point for analysis is that of 3rd Armored Cavalry Regiment's campaign in Tal Afar in 2005 to 2006.

There are vast resources concerning the U.S. Army's tactical COIN approaches in Vietnam from 1965 to 1973. Research materials pertaining to the Vietnam case study found in Chapter 3 have been limited to a few key pieces to preserve a focused scope. Several primary sources were utilized in developing the basis for the Vietnam case study. Andrew Birtle's *U.S. Army Counterinsurgency and Contingency Operations Doctrine: 1942-1976* outlined the evolution of the Army's approach to COIN during the Vietnam War. Chapter 8 of Birtle's book was useful in understanding the concepts by which Army battalion and brigade-sized elements countered insurgent threats during various phases of the war. It discussed the predominant COIN approach that American tactical echelons utilized at the onset of major hostilities in 1966:

> Switch from harassment to sustained offensive operations, exploiting the steady growth of American combat and logistical power to destroy the enemy's major forces and bases. Meanwhile, the [South] Vietnamese, under the cover of American operations and with some direct American help, would undertake pacification operations in selected areas. Finally, after the enemy's main forces had been broken and dispersed, the allies would mop up the remaining insurgent infrastructure and solidify the government's presence in the countryside,

24

introducing more permanent political and socioeconomic reforms to strengthen the government's presence and redress the causes of discontent.[12]

Additionally, the book conveyed the methods by which tactical units designed COIN operations during the late 1960s. Just as today's FM 3-24 doctrinal construct involves application of the Clear-Hold-Build, Combined Action, and Limited Support approaches to COIN, General Westmoreland (commander of Military Assistance Command, Vietnam) outlined the tactics and procedures he wanted to be executed in Vietnam. Westmoreland's guidance created the Vietnam-era COIN paradigm of "Search-Destroy-Clear-Hold-Secure."[13] Search-and-Destroy operations were the first operations executed in this COIN approach and were loosely similar to today's cordon and search and zone clearance missions. The second phase was "Clear and Hold." These operations, lower on the scale of lethality than search and destroy missions, were applied as "condition-setters" for areas that were earmarked for pacification. The final phase of Westmoreland's approach to COIN was "Secure." These operations usually offered no distinction from "Clear and Hold," but were designed to reinforce security gains in a cleared area and to facilitate the reintroduction of government, essential civil services, and law enforcement.[14] The comprehensive Vietnam-era COIN approach of "Search-Destroy-Clear-Hold-Secure" can be viewed as the doctrinal precedent of the modern Clear-Hold-Build approach.

The second key source concerning tactical COIN design in Vietnam and its relevance to current operations is a scholarly paper entitled *Insurgency and Counterinsurgency in the 21st Century: Reconceptualizing Threat and Response*. This paper was co-written by defense strategists Steven Metz and Raymond Millen. The authors contend that the United States Army, despite a long history of COIN, was ill-prepared doctrinally, conceptually, and organizationally for the war that it faced when it began large scale operations in Vietnam in 1965.[15] Metz and Millen argue that at the time of Vietnam, "the Army, at least at the senior level, placed little stress on the mundane but vital aspects of COIN, such as training the South Vietnamese security forces, village pacification, local self-defense, and rooting out insurgent political cadres."[16] The stance that these two authors share indicates that despite having established practices for COIN operations as outlined by Birtle (Search-Destroy-Clear-Hold-Secure), the Army was not following the spirit of its doctrine or the basic historical tenets of counterinsurgencies.

A further important argument from this source justifies the rationale for this thesis: the sting from botched experiences in Vietnam drove the U.S. Army to bury any further movement to ready itself for future protracted counterinsurgencies. As a result, the lessons learned by the tactical units conducting COIN operations through the late 1960s and early 1970s were largely abandoned by the U.S. Army in its departure from the villages and jungles of Southeast Asia. This supports the two authors' contention that the Vietnam-era Army was not a learning organization. Failure to adopt the lessons of Vietnam meant that Army's next generation would not benefit from the practical COIN experiences gained from 1965 to 1973:

> the U.S. military, and particularly the Army, was so disillusioned by Vietnam that it has since kept insurgency and counterinsurgency at arm's length. When it could not be avoided, it was folded into, even hidden, in other concepts such as low intensity conflict, Foreign Internal Defense, and now stability operations and support operations. Given the centrality of insurgency and counterinsurgency in the contemporary strategic environment, the Army must transcend this hesitancy and accord these forms of conflict the priority they merit in strategy, operational thinking, doctrine, concept development, and force development.[17]

The final key source utilized in the study of COIN operations in Vietnam is John A. Nagl's *Counterinsurgency Lessons from Malaya and Vietnam: Learning to Eat Soup with a Knife*. The book was published in 2002--several months after the Global War on Terror was initiated but well in advance of the insurgent quagmire that emerged in Iraq the following year. Nagl gives critical attention to the U.S. Army's lessons learned conducting COIN operations in Vietnam and the theory behind the design and planning of such operations.

Nagl contrasts in detail how COIN operations in Malaya and Vietnam were approached by the British and the U.S. military, respectively. He references the direct and indirect operational approaches--terms that are still used today in the elements of operational design as outlined in FM 3-0. Nagl adequately defines both operational approaches. He demonstrates that the direct approach is reminiscent of the traditional Western practice of attacking the armed forces and adversarial factions of your opponent outright. He defines the indirect approach as programmed efforts to separate the critical mass (the populace) from the insurgents.[18] His argument is clear that the indirect approach is preferred because it adequately addresses the center of gravity of a COIN environment: control of the local populace. Nagl cites a dated but oft-referenced analogy made by Mao Zedong that likens fighting insurgents to separating fish from water.

> They [insurgent and support elements] may be said to constitute the head and the body of a fish. The third element is the population and this represents the water in which the fish swims. Fish vary from place to place in accordance with the water in which they are designed to live, and the same can be said of subversive organizations. If a fish has got to be destroyed it can be attacked directly by rod or net, providing it is in the sort of position which gives these methods a chance of success. But if rod and net cannot succeed by themselves it may be necessary to do something to the water which will force the fish into a position where it can be caught.[19]

The parallels that exist between Mao's view of gaining support and control of the populace as the lynchpin to success are not overlooked in FM 3-24. Additionally, most

contemporary COIN theorists, including Nagl, David Kilcullen, and Andrew
Krepinevich, have embraced Mao's theory. Thus, it may be considered that ultimately
Mao's essential orientation to population helped to shape the BSP in 2007.

Another important aspect of Nagl's book is his indictment of the U.S. Army's
inability to learn from the Vietnam War. He is in agreement with the assessment of Metz
and Millen that the Army did not benefit from the lessons which Vietnam presented. Nagl
contends that the Army was poor at adaptation and failed in most accounts to deviate
from the inadequate doctrine that existed at the time--doctrine that was largely based on
conventional and linear force structure and combating a like-structured enemy.[20] He cites
the failure of the Army in securing progress in Vietnam as proof of its lack of
organizational learning. Nagl believes that the U.S. Army remained enemy-oriented
throughout the war and never grasped the fundamentals of COIN warfare. Additionally,
the idea of having secondary echelons to hold gains and rebuild damages sustained
during offensive operations escaped Army leaders from strategic to tactical levels
through most of the war.[21] It could easily be argued that the U.S. Army maintained the
same offensive mindset when Iraq was ripe with insurgency in late 2003. This argument
itself is indicative of the Army's failure to institutionalize appropriate COIN lessons
following the Vietnam War.

The second historical COIN study is more recent. Since there were no protracted,
tactical COIN operations conducted by the U.S. Army from 1973 to 2003, it is necessary
to analyze the initial COIN operations of OIF. The study of the first years of the war in
Iraq is designed to bridge the gap from the conclusion of the Vietnam War to the start of
the BSP and the formal beginnings of C-H-B doctrine. Since FM 3-24 was not released

28

until the end of 2006, it is important to analyze the first three years of OIF to understand the linkages from protracted COIN in Vietnam to operations in Iraq.

The case study concerning early COIN operations in Iraq details the actions of 3rd Armored Cavalry Regiment (ACR) in the city of Tal Afar during Operation Restoring Rights, conducted throughout the summer of 2005. A declassified After Action Report (AAR) was the primary source in analyzing this case study. While the AAR's chapter involving COIN planning still remains classified, the unclassified materials provided the general methodology that the 3rd ACR utilized to fashion an ad hoc C-H-B-type tactical campaign. It was this unit's approach to COIN that President George W. Bush cited in a March 2006 speech. He alluded to 3rd ACR's execution of the principals of clearing, holding, and building even before it had become an accepted term.

> The ability of al Qaeda and its associates to retake Tal Afar was an example of something we saw elsewhere in Iraq. We recognized the problem, and we changed our strategy. Instead of coming in and removing the terrorists, and then moving on, the Iraqi government and the coalition adopted a new approach called clear, hold, and build. This new approach was made possible because of the significant gains made in training large numbers of highly capable Iraqi security forces. Under this new approach, Iraq and coalition -- Iraqi and coalition forces would clear a city of the terrorists, leave well-trained Iraqi units behind to hold the city, and work with local leaders to build the economic and political infrastructure Iraqis need to live in freedom.[22]

The study of 3rd ACR's COIN operations in Tal Afar highlights the Army's maturing ability to conduct successful COIN operations following its failures in Vietnam. Likewise, this study frames the conditions which demanded the Army's COIN doctrinal revisions and implementation of the BSP in early 2007.

Contemporary Counterinsurgency Operations Resources

One of the most enlightening resources regarding the Army's modern approach to COIN operations came from a 2005 article in *Foreign Affairs* magazine. Andrew Krepinevich wrote an articulate synopsis of how the Army could defeat the insurgency that had spread throughout Iraq by 2005. It is more than interesting that this article, entitled simply "How to Win in Iraq" was written before Secretary Rice presented the concept of "clear, hold, and build" in October of that year. Krepinevich argues that a defined end state (something that he felt the U.S. did not have at the time) is the singularly most important facet in the COIN environment.[23] This is key for consideration in this thesis because it represents the penultimate fundamental of the modern operational design model.

Krepinevich's suggestion on how the Army could best approach COIN operations in Iraq is most insightful. He presents the concept of the "oil spot" strategy--an approach somewhat similar to the C-H-B method publicized just weeks later when Secretary Rice presented her concept to the Senate Foreign Relations Committee.

> U.S. and Iraqi forces should adopt an "oil-spot strategy" in Iraq, which is essentially the opposite approach. Rather than focusing on killing insurgents, they should concentrate on providing security and opportunity to the Iraqi people, thereby denying insurgents the popular support they need. Since the U.S. and Iraqi armies cannot guarantee security to all of Iraq simultaneously, they should start by focusing on certain key areas and then, over time, broadening the effort-- hence the image of an expanding oil spot. Such a strategy would have a good chance of success. But it would require a protracted commitment of U.S. resources, a willingness to risk more casualties in the short term, and an enduring U.S. presence in Iraq, albeit at far lower force levels than are engaged at present.[24]

It would seem that the theory proposed by Krepinevich feeds off the Galulan and Maoist models for executing COIN, supports the precepts of C-H-B, and also supports the logic and design which shaped the BSP.

Krepinevich also offers another incisive point regarding the Army's collective mindset several years into the war in Vietnam.

> During the Vietnam War, U.S. strategy focused on killing insurgents at the expense of winning hearts and minds. This search-and-destroy strategy ultimately failed, but it evidently continues to exert a strong pull on the U.S. military, as indicated by statements like that of a senior army commander in Iraq who declared, "[I] don't think we will put much energy into trying the old saying, 'win the hearts and minds.' I don't look at it as one of the metrics of success." Having left the business of waging counterinsurgency warfare over 30 years ago, the U.S. military is running the risk of failing to do what is needed most (win Iraqis' hearts and minds) in favor of what it has traditionally done best (seek out the enemy and destroy him).[25]

Krepinevich's article roughly outlines the same construct and doctrinal principles for executing COIN operations under the C-H-B approach. His insight, given the situation in Iraq in late 2005 and the eventual implementation of the BSP, may have indeed been considered throughout 2006 by governmental and military planners.

One of the principal documents that guided this thesis is an essay considered to be the genesis of the BSP itself. Lieutenant Colonel Douglas Ollivant and First Lieutenant Eric Chewning created the blueprint for the development of the BSP in early 2006. Their essay, "Producing Victory: Rethinking Conventional Forces in Counterinsurgency Operations," was recognized by the U.S. Army Combined Arms Center as the winner of a special essay contest on countering insurgency, referenced earlier. The essay, based on analysis of experiences in Iraq and historical COIN lessons, argued that the U.S. Army maneuver battalion is the prime unit for executing modern, urban COIN operations. They contend that while smaller echelons (such as companies and special operations detachments) have the capability to execute successful COIN operations, their lack of a purpose-oriented staff and organic enablers prevents them from prosecuting action independent of their immediate higher headquarters. The counterargument is made for

31

echelons beyond battalion level. The authors feel that brigade and divisional staff structures and associated enablers are essential to facilitating tactical COIN operations, but their inability to directly operate amongst the populace prevents them from serving as the optimal unit of employment in the urban COIN operational environment.[26] This contention that the battalion is the optimal echelon for conducting COIN operations is echoed in Galula's statement below:

> The area will be divided into sectors and sub-sectors, each with its own static unit. The subdivision should be carried out down to the level of the basic unit of counterinsurgency warfare: the largest unit whose leader is in direct and continuous contact with the population. This is the most important unit in counterinsurgency operations, the level where most of the practical problems arise, and in each case where the war is won or lost.[27]

The Ollivant and Chewning essay was also extremely insightful in determining why the doctrinal concepts of operational design and campaign planning have critical relevancy at lower tactical levels. If battalions are to be tasked to execute protracted COIN operations, as they were during the BSP, they must have a basic framework to design such operations tactically.

Another key source for understanding tactical level COIN operations in Iraq from 2007-2008 was Linda Robinson's recently published book entitled *Tell Me How This Ends: General David Petraeus and the Search for a Way Out of Iraq*. Robinson's résumé is robust and it seems that her journalism experience is matched only by a willingness to immerse herself in the environment on which she reports.[28] Her time spent in Iraq is comparable to many Soldiers of the GWOT era, and as a result her material is well supported and accurate.

Robinson's book details the deteriorating situation in Iraq in early 2006 and lays out the conditions which necessitated the BSP and the necessary troop surge in Iraq in

2007. Her book discusses the initial applications of C-H-B in Baghdad, ranging from the first operation in the Adamiyah security district to the East Rashid district that had become the last bastion for AQIZ in the capital city. Two of her chapters yield important insights pertaining to the C-H-B operations by battalions in these security districts and illustrate how these units designed C-H-B operations in some of the most challenging neighborhoods in Baghdad. Robinson points out that the United States Government's *National Strategy for Victory in Iraq*, issued in November of 2005, included the concept of C-H-B on both military and diplomatic fronts. She argues that this strategic approach received inadequate attention and resources and thus failed until the start of the troop surge in 2007.[29]

Chapter Conclusion

The literature review has established the feedstock of references upon which the analysis of this thesis has been developed. These sources encompass doctrine, historical C-H-B operations, the roots of COIN efforts in Iraq, and modern methodologies concerning tactical design of COIN operations. The following chapter outlines the counterinsurgency understanding and its application from the Vietnam-era U.S. Army. The purpose of this analysis is to illustrate how dated tactical COIN theory has shaped our contemporary doctrine for conducting COIN operations, despite the Army's failure to absorb the applicable lessons from the Vietnam War.

---

[1]Department of the Army, FM 3-0, 3-1, 3-2.

[2]Ibid., 3-1.

[3]Ibid., 3-8.

[4]Ibid., 2-11.

[5]Ibid.

[6]Department of the Army, FM 3-24, 4-1.

[7]Ibid., 4-2.

[8]Ibid., 5-18.

[9]Ibid.

[10]Ibid., 1-8.

[11]David Galula, *Counterinsurgency Warfare: Theory and Practice* (London: Praeger, 1964), 107-118.

[12]Andrew J. Birtle, *U.S. Army Counterinsurgency and Contingency Operations Doctrine: 1942-1976* (Washington, DC: Center for Military History, 2006), 366.

[13]Ibid., 368-369.

[14]Ibid., 368-372.

[15]Steven Metz and Raymond Millen, "Insurgency and Counterinsurgency in the 21st Century: Reconceptualizing Threat and Response" (Scholarly Essay, Strategic Studies Institute, Carlisle, PA 2004), 10.

[16]Ibid.

[17]Ibid., 34.

[18]John A. Nagl, *Counterinsurgency Lessons from Malaya and Vietnam: Learning to Eat Soup with a Knife* (Westport, CT: Praeger Publishers, 2002), 27-29.

[19]Frank Kitson, *Low Intensity Operations: Subversion, Insurgency and Peacekeeping* (London, England: Faber and Faber, 1971), 49.

[20]Nagl, 155.

[21]Ibid., 155-156.

[22]The White House, News Release, March 20, 2006, http://www.whitehouse.gov/news/releases/2006/03/20060320-7.html (accessed December 6, 2008).

[23]Andrew F. Krepinevich, Jr. "How to Win in Iraq," *Foreign Affairs* 84, no. 5 (September/October 2005), 87.

[24]Ibid., 88-89.

[25]Ibid., 93.

[26]Ollivant and Chewning, 50-51.

[27]Galula, 110-111.

[28]Linda Robinson, *Tell Me How This Ends: General David Petraeus and the Search for a Way Out of Iraq* (New York, NY: PublicAffairs, 2008), 411.

[29]Ibid., 18-19.

CHAPTER 3

THE ARMY RE-LEARNS COUNTERINSURGENCY

Case Study 1: The Counterinsurgency Culture of Vietnam

The purpose of this case study is twofold. The first is to outline the general framework within which the U.S. Army executed its COIN efforts during the Vietnam War from 1965 to 1973. The second and more important purpose is to highlight the major lessons regarding COIN doctrine and practice which the U.S. Army failed to inculcate in the haste of its mental and physical departure from Southeast Asia. Since the U.S. Army was not involved in any protracted COIN operations involving committed conventional forces from the end of that conflict to the start of the Global War on Terror, and did not develop any meaningful COIN doctrine upon the costly base of the Vietnam experience, it is crucial for us to revisit those last historical data points, frozen in time, to understand how the Army's COIN methodology evolved.

Overview of Counterinsurgency Practices in Vietnam

The year 1965 was a turning point for the U.S. Army in Vietnam. The worsening insurgency, unable to be stemmed over the decade prior, demanded that the President and military leaders initiate a significant shifting of political and military strategy. Prior to 1965 the U.S. Army's main efforts involved delegitimizing the communist insurgents whose ideology had taken root in North Vietnam. These efforts involved pacifying population areas, relocating citizens and entire villages suspected of abetting insurgents, and conducting limited Foreign Internal Defense (FID) operations. While these approaches offered some merit, namely that they required only limited commitment and support from the U.S. Government, it was obvious that a more intensive approach was necessary to combat the insurgency effectively. What emerged in 1965 was a direct method of military engagement that included the full-scale commitment of U.S. ground forces tasked to conduct offensive and counter-guerrilla operations.

The general strategy that developed in Vietnam with the commitment of conventional U.S. Army formations is reminiscent of Andrew Krepinevich's oil spot theory. The Army sought to revitalize the French "ink spot" approach of securing population centers and gradually expanding into the countryside when conditions allowed. The U.S. Army's spin on this proven COIN approach was to blend deliberate offensive operations, extensive population control measures, and robust civil action programs all aimed at reestablishing and expanding South Vietnamese governmental control.[1] The problem with this approach was that many of the insurgent concentrations and safe havens were outside of the territorial borders of Vietnam in the neighboring countries of Laos and Cambodia. Targeting these insurgent safe havens proved exceptionally problematic--in fact, incursions into most of these areas were diplomatically forbidden. The ink spot approach was largely limited in efficacy because the ability to expand the spot was constrained by the geometry of international borders.

A second, internal problem for the implementation of this strategy was the Army senior leadership's predisposition to offensive employment of its forces against military targets; these leaders did not accept the critical value of the population as the true center of gravity. Simply put, their focal point remained oriented on neutralizing the adversaries of the South Vietnamese Government. This mindset prevented U.S. efforts from achieving Mao's and Galula's principal COIN fundamental of winning the popular fight.

37

The U.S. Army's overarching goal was the destruction of enemy combatants and resources--a contradiction to the historically regarded goal of securing the support of the populace. The Army's failure to understand the dynamics of the operating environment resulted in its inability to positively influence the Vietnamese populace. This also meant that it could not accomplish the objective of defeating the enemy insurgency because the enemy had in large part become the populace. The mindset of the Army's senior leadership was a "Jominian vision of the object of warfare as the destruction of enemy forces"[2] according to author and OIF veteran John Nagl. Nagl expanded this perception by stating the following:

> This concept was so deeply ingrained in the army's leaders that they refused to listen to innovators from below who were convinced that the army's concept was not just ineffective but actually counterproductive in the new kind of warfare the nation faced in Vietnam.[3]

A second COIN approach was proposed to minimize the dangers of the escalating war in Vietnam. Retired Army General turned Ambassador Maxwell Taylor developed a strategy for U.S. Army forces to guard vital nodes, bases, and population centers while the Army of the Republic of Vietnam (ARVN) would maintain primacy for conducting COIN operations in the countryside. This concept is reminiscent of "operational overwatch" utilized in modern U.S. Army COIN operations. Operational overwatch involves securing key facilities and infrastructure while providing material and direct security assistance when required by the host nation. This concept typically involves establishing the host nation's forces "in the lead" with respect to establishing security. General Taylor's "enclave approach" was widely dismissed by the operational commanders in Vietnam. Their enemy-centric mindset, coupled with the immature and ineffective ARVN forces, contributed to the belief that a passive defense against North

Vietnamese aggression would only serve to worsen the problem.[4]

The Cold War dominated strategic and operational level design, the rage in

central Europe, predisposed the U.S. Army to failure in Vietnam. Foremost was the lack

of succinct strategic and operational end states. Politicians and senior military leaders

were enamored with enemy body counts and failed to properly identify the terminal

conditions of success. Efforts to defeat adversarial elements, control terrain, and gain the

support of the Vietnamese populace were not synchronized, resulting in piecemeal

progress with temporary successes. Operational commanders yielded little autonomy to

the lower tactical echelons, preferring to mass air and ground power against suspected

enemy concentrations. David Galula's concepts of dispersing forces throughout insurgent

bases and utilizing the lowest tactical formations to conduct COIN operations had largely

been ignored.[5] The senior leadership's failure to realize how counterinsurgencies are won

illustrates the fundamental error in the operational design of the Vietnam War. Politically

motivated strategic decisions certainly affected the war adversely, but the operational

mindset of Army leaders and paradigms of Army conventional tactics and operations

were the true catalysts for failure. In summary, the Army's ignorance in recognizing the

nature of the insurgency and their inability to frame this operational problem correctly

correlated to the application of failed tactics by the U.S. Army from 1965 to the end of

the Vietnam War.

While the burden of guilt for the failed COIN efforts in Vietnam rests upon

leaders above the tactical level, there were numerous tactical mistakes which exacerbated

the situation. As discussed in the previous chapter, the prevailing tactical design for counter-guerrilla operations in the late 1960s was the "Search-Destroy-Clear-Hold-Secure" approach. This approach did not exist in U.S. Army doctrine but was rather a design of General Westmoreland.[6] Despite this fact, the approach offered a rudimentary architecture for tactical echelons to design basic COIN operations. The approach was first utilized at brigade and battalion level beginning in 1966. Operations such as Attleboro (a brigade action conducted by the 196th Light Infantry Brigade from September through November of 1966) were designed based on the concept. Operation Attleboro was the first brigade-level action since the commitment of entire combat formations in 1965, and "proved that large-scale [tactical] operations . . . have a place in modern counterinsurgency warfare."[7] It would serve as the model by which future COIN tactical actions in Vietnam would be designed. The problem with execution of "Search-Destroy-Clear-Hold-Secure," as proven during Attleboro, was that the fifth phase in this approach, "Secure," was usually ignored by tactical units.

Operation Cedar Falls occurred during January of 1967. It was designed to eradicate Vietcong irregulars and their support bases located immediately north of Saigon. This operation was born out of the tactical successes achieved during Operation Attleboro just weeks prior. Operation Cedar Falls became a testament to the U.S. Army's ignorance of COIN warfare theory.

The operation was founded on the tenets of COIN: its purpose was to disintegrate the command, control, and logistics infrastructure of the Vietcong forces closest to the South Vietnam capitol of Saigon. Cedar Falls was tactically designed to achieve this result through two measures. First, U.S. Army forces would separate the insurgents from the populated villages north of Saigon. Secondly, forces would neutralize the insurgents' continued ability to utilize these population centers as support bases.[8] The design did not translate successfully into tactical execution however. While historians typically regard Operation Cedar Falls as one of the more successful U.S. operations of the Vietnam War, tactical failures during the operation eventually created conditions for operational and strategic failure in the region. Aerial saturation bombing, wholesale population relocation, and forced reeducation temporarily incapacitated the Vietcong but had no lasting positive effects. Likewise, the inability or unwillingness of tactical forces to physically secure the gains from the operation contributed to a fleeting success. Finally, the forced relocation of over 6000 Vietnamese local nationals during Operation Cedar Falls created tremendous dissidence among the South Vietnamese population. While the U.S. Army fumbled to operate within the fundamentals of COIN warfare, its efforts proved entirely counterproductive as thousands of South Vietnamese citizens lost confidence in their wobbly government. Operation Cedar Falls highlights the failed tactical design and execution of U.S. Army counterinsurgency actions from 1965 to 1973.

Post-Vietnam Counterinsurgency Culture in the Army

While analysis of U.S. Army COIN operations following 1965 offers significant insight, it is equally important to analyze the counterinsurgency mindset of the Army following Vietnam. It is unusual for a military institution to endure more than a decade of committed warfare only to emerge as a less capable organization in that type of warfare. Author John Nagl believes that this is exactly what the U.S. Army experienced in the years following the Vietnam War. Nagl states the following:

> In marked contrast the British army in the evolutionary development of counterinsurgency learning since the Malayan Emergency, the U.S. Army has failed to form a consensus on the lessons of Vietnam and has not accepted the

41

idea that revolutionary war requires a qualitatively different response from the conventional warfare it knows so well to fight.[9]

Dr. Richard Downie, a retired U.S. Army officer and Director of the Center for Hemispheric Defense Studies, shares Nagl's perspective on the U.S. Army's failure to leave Vietnam as more COIN-capable organization. His doctoral research in 1998 discovered "no significant conceptual change to the Army's counterinsurgency doctrine in the post-Vietnam War era."[10] He expounded on this premise by stating that "the Army was well aware of deficiencies in its counterinsurgency doctrine" but "did not change its doctrine to correct or resolve these deficiencies."[11] He summarized his thoughts by stating the following: "The Army did not learn from its Vietnam War and other LIC [Low Intensity Conflict] experiences."[12]

In *Learning to Eat Soup with a Knife*, Nagl illustrates the sentiment that the U.S. Army held for COIN operations following its departure from Vietnam. He states that,

> Rather than squarely face up to the fact that army counterinsurgency doctrine had failed in Vietnam, the [United States] army decided that the United States should no longer involve itself in counterinsurgency operations. The "Weinberger doctrine" of 1983 made such involvement less likely by creating a series of tests that in practice precluded American participation in any wars that did not allow full exploitation of American advantages in technology and firepower.[13]

This statement helps us understand how such experiences from Vietnam could become forgotten so easily: instead of facing the problem of how to fight such wars effectively, the Army followed its civilian leaders' policy guidance and assumed that we would never engage in such wars again. While Nagl and Downie share the opinion that there was abject failure by the U.S. Army to learn from its experiences conducting COIN operations in Vietnam, the Army did indeed revise some aspects of its COIN doctrine. The Army published FM 90-8, *Counterguerrilla Operations*, in 1986. FM 90-8 was the lone manual to emerge from the Army's experiences in Vietnam a decade prior in which

COIN is addressed in terms of a conventional force mission. The manual does not present

any striking differences in approach from what is found in the 2006 version of FM 3-24,

Counterinsurgency. There is one shocking omission however: not one historical vignette

or mention of the Vietnam War exists in FM 90-8. How could the Army of the mid-1980s

fail to incorporate the painful lessons from its recent past? Perhaps the psychological

stigma of leaving Vietnam without definitive victory was still too great. It could also

have been the policy paradigm that existed at the time: the Army viewed its experience in

Vietnam as an anomaly--a type of war never to be waged again. For whatever reason, the

failure to acknowledge or reflect doctrinally upon the victories and defeats of its often

dismal COIN experience in Vietnam meant that the post-Vietnam Army was no better

equipped to operate in such an environment than its predecessors.

It is worth taking a brief look into the limited COIN doctrine that was published

in the 1980s. FM 90-8 was the only real attempt by the Army to address conventional

force COIN theory following Vietnam. The manual presents minor indication that

valuable irregular warfare lessons were in fact internalized following Vietnam. For

instance, paragraph 1-14 of FM 90-8 lists the following principles that tactical units must

incorporate in the design and execution of counterguerrilla operations:

(1) Be appropriate--response is appropriate to the level of threat and activity.

(2) Be justifiable--actions taken are justifiable in the eyes of the host country's
population and the U.S. public.

(3) Use minimum force--the goal is to restrict the use of force and the level of
commitment to the minimum feasible to accomplish the mission. However, the
principle of minimum necessary force does not always imply minimum necessary
troops. A large number of men deployed at the right time may enable a
commander to use less force than he might otherwise have done, or even to avoid

43

using any force at all. Commanders must, however, keep in mind that a peaceful situation could become hostile because of the provocative display of an overlarge force. Doing too much may be a greater danger than doing too little.

(4) Do maximum benefit--U.S. forces should select operations so they accomplish positive benefit for the population. If this is not possible then the operational concept is wrong and should not be executed.

(5) Do minimum damage--U.S. forces ensure that operations preclude unnecessary damage to facilities, activities, and resources. Since this is almost an impossibility, compensation for any damage to property must be made and the property restored, as much as possible, to its original state. In any case, a major consideration is to plan activities to limit damage.[14]

Each of these principles from FM 90-8 is represented in FM 3-24.[15]

FM 90-8 does delve somewhat into the practice of COIN. The delineation between "counter-guerrilla" and "counterinsurgent" is clarified early in the manual with the following statement.

There is a difference in the terms counterinsurgency and counterguerrilla. The internal defense and development (IDAD) program is geared to counter the whole insurgency. It does this through alleviating conditions which may cause insurgency. This program, which addresses both the populace and the insurgent, can be termed counterinsurgency. Counterguerrilla operations are geared to the active military element of the insurgent movement only. To this end, counterguerrilla operations are viewed as a supporting component of the counterinsurgency effort.[16]

The manual states that the preferred method for the U.S. Army to execute COIN operations is through FID. This is notable because it implied an unwillingness to commit tactical formations in a protracted manner to combat an insurgency. This mentality may be attributed to the "Weinberger Doctrine" that governed the U.S. Military throughout the 1980s. This doctrine, noted earlier, stated that military forces would only participate in conflicts that allowed for the maximum application of its capabilities--specifically in regards to technological advancements and overwhelming combat power.

Counterinsurgency operations did not fit this mold because the nature of such conflict did not inherently stress mass and technology.

The entire Chapter 3 of FM 90-8 is devoted to COIN doctrine. One of the most interesting premises of the chapter is that the "COIN Program" (largely analogous to a Joint Campaign Plan in contemporary doctrine) was presented as being the responsibility of the host nation government and not the U.S. Government. This meant that employment of U.S. Armed Force in a "Foreign COIN Program" would allow the Army to focus on prosecution of the counter-guerrilla fight and not the "nation building" skills of contemporary COIN operations. FM 90-8 does indicate that stability-type operations are required in order for military efforts to succeed:

> U.S. forces committed to FID in the host country have a dual mission. First, they must defeat or neutralize the guerrilla militarily so the host country government can begin or resume functioning in previously contested or guerrilla-controlled areas. Second, they must support the overall COIN program by conducting noncombat operations to provide an environment where the host country government can win the trust and support of its people and ultimately become self-sustaining. Both aspects of the COIN mission are of equal importance and are usually conducted simultaneously.

> A common mistake made by FID forces when trying to gain popular support is that they sometimes win popular support only for themselves. The commander must ensure that popular support, in the end, is for the host country government. Credit for successful campaigns against the guerrillas, or programs to help the people, should go to the host country government and not to the FID force commander.[17]

One of the most glaring omissions in FM 90-8 was doctrine regarding how to design COIN operations. While the Army had codified some COIN theory, no doctrine existed that shaped how U.S. Army tactical echelons should design, plan, and execute such operations. The absence of such doctrine still exists in large part today.

A final notable aspect of FM 90-8 is the mention that U.S. Army brigades are the primary echelon for conducting tactical operations in a COIN operating environment.[18] This statement indicates that the offense-centric culture of the Vietnam-era Army had permeated the Army's next generation of COIN doctrine. The Army had failed to realize Galula's notion that COIN operations are best conducted by the largest unit that still maintains the ability to independently operate amongst the populace. Galula's belief is that it is at this level that a counterinsurgency is won or lost.[19] Field Manual 90-8 failed to address this organizational concept. The brigade structure of the Vietnam-era may have afforded the Army the most efficient means for operating in Southeast Asia in major combat operations, but it did not prove capable of effectively conducing COIN operations, as evident during the 196th Light Infantry Brigade's execution of Operation Attleboro. In overlooking battalions as the prime units of employment for conducting COIN operations, FM 90-8 failed to recognize that counterinsurgency is a fight won at the lowest tactical levels.

The U.S. Army emerged from Vietnam without reflecting on the past counterinsurgency conflict, and was therefore not oriented towards preparing for future COIN warfare. The Army failed to grasp the art of COIN during the Vietnam War and left as ignorant a force as when it arrived en masse in 1965. The fact that no pragmatic COIN doctrine emerged in the era following Vietnam is hard to fathom. As the Cold War raced through the 1980s, it seems inconceivable that the U.S. Army had not prepared its conventional forces for the potential of having to combat Communist proxies throughout the world, as they had in Vietnam. The Army, driven by the Weinberger Doctrine and the escalation of spending on a conventional force oriented toward a Soviet Army in Europe, had distanced itself from the potential of having to relive its painful past. The failure to shift the culture of the Army following the Vietnam War justifies one of Nagl's final impressions when he states that, "By failing to learn the lessons of Vietnam, the U.S. Army continued to prepare itself to fight the wrong war."[20] One might go beyond this statement as well: the collapse of the Soviet Union (1989) and the quick victory in Desert Storm (1991) served to reinforce every Army conviction regarding major combat operations, and also reinforced the associated thinking that Vietnam-style COIN warfare was an unrepeatable historical anomaly.

In summary, the COIN lessons extracted from nearly fifteen years of conflict in Vietnam are myriad. The list below, developed by Robert W. Komer, captures the major themes that the U.S. Army should have, but did not learn from the Vietnam War. Thirty years later it would take a progressive unit to grind its way through a complex insurgency in the city of Tal Afar, Iraq to finally "turn the corner" and put the painful lessons of a failed counterinsurgency campaign in Vietnam to rest.

Photo Removed Due to Copyright Restrictions

Figure 4.   Comprehensive List of Army COIN Lessons from Vietnam
Source: Robert W. Komer, *Bureaucracy Does Its Thing* (Santa Monica, CA: Rand, 1972), v-xii.

Case Study 2: Tal Afar: The Genesis of Clear-Hold-Build

The U.S. Army was not entirely out of the COIN business during the twenty eight years that passed from the conclusion of the Vietnam War to the start of OIF. However, the end of major combat operations in Iraq during 2003 presented the first full-scale commitment of conventional forces to combat an insurgency since Vietnam. The insurgency, which developed in Iraq in that year, required the Army to reeducate itself on COIN doctrine, principles, and practices. This process was not easy. The Desert Storm victory in Kuwait and southern Iraq in 1991 prompted President George H. W. Bush to state that "By God, we've licked the Vietnam syndrome once and for all."[21] The elder Bush's son, President George W. Bush, quickly came to discover that the successes of the 96-hour ground campaign of his father's war in Iraq would not be so easily duplicated in his war. The younger President Bush also arrived at the stark realization that the "Vietnam syndrome" was metastasizing.

The insurgency in Iraq, which began in earnest over the latter half of 2003, can be attributed in part to the orders mandating de-Baathification and dissolution of the Iraqi army by the Coalition Provisional Authority. The dynamics of the insurgency were complex. Shiite, Sunni, and Kurdish insurgent movements originated in the vacuum created when Saddam Hussein's dictatorship collapsed. Several foreign nations fueled these movements and intensified the operating environment. The first litmus test of the U.S. Army's protracted counterinsurgency fighting ability following Vietnam had begun.

Tal Afar, a city of nearly 200,000 inhabitants, sits in northwest Iraq 35 miles from Mosul and 40 miles east of the Syrian border. This city harbored a growing group of Sunni dissidents throughout 2004. The 3rd Armored Cavalry Regiment (ACR) arrived in

March of 2005, already a seasoned combat unit from its deployment during the invasion

of Iraq in 2003. The 3rd ACR quickly realized that the insurgent movements in Iraq,

particularly in Tal Afar, had matured to a perilous magnitude. This situational

understanding drove the unit to adopt major tactical changes from the "kill or capture"

approach utilized during the unit's first deployment in 2003.[22]

The 3rd ACR recognized the necessity to transition from conventional offensive

and defensive operations to more asymmetric ones. The leadership of the unit was in

concert with the theory shared by Mao and Galula that the center of gravity of an

insurgency is the populace itself. While other units throughout Iraq were slowly coming

to the same realization, the 3rd ACR acted. The unit's "new counterinsurgency thinking,

officially termed 'clear, hold, and build,' explicitly recognized that the solution is only

partly military and that the lethal, somewhat indiscriminate use of force so productive in

a conventional battlefield, here is essentially counterproductive" according to McCone,

Scott, and Mastroianni.[23]

What was the operating environment in Iraq circa early 2005? To start, the

insurgency was shifting from "strategic defense" to "strategic stalemate" within Mao

Zedong's Theory of Protracted War.[24] Simply put, the insurgent movements had

graduated from latent, formative stages to become overt and action-oriented. The U.S

Army was still largely ignorant of the magnitude of these movements. It was functioning

with a linear mindset--offensive and defensive actions were the preferred themes of

operation. Additionally, there was no institutional impetus to shift this paradigm. The

venerable FM 90-8, *Counterguerrilla Operations*, was the only manual available to

outline conventional COIN principles. In short, the Army had woefully failed to adapt to the changing operating environment and did not meet the threat of the insurgency which had become painfully visible by the start of 2005.

The 3rd ACR was one of the few units that shared an understanding of the operating environment. The unit began Operation Restoring Rights in Tal Afar in June of 2005. Restoring Rights can be considered the first tactical COIN campaign of OIF. The unit broke the paradigm of the Army's predisposition towards lethal offensive action and shifted its focus to applying the theories and practices of COIN warfare. Gone was the direct approach of applying force to neutralize targets--the 3rd ACR understood that they could not kill their way out of the insurgency in Tal Afar. The unit instead designed a tactical construct that specifically addressed the root of the problem and not just the perpetrators.

The 3rd ACR's first step in designing their tactical COIN approach was to define the overarching problem and develop the end state that their operations would work to achieve. The end state which this regiment embraced was "that the bulk of the town's people would side with them, provide actionable intelligence, and make the dirty work of cleaning out the insurgents worthwhile."[25] The center of gravity (COG) that the 3rd ACR identified to achieve this end state was winning the trust and support of the residents of Tal Afar--a COG that was equally vital to the insurgents attempting to retain control of the city. The unit's approach to tipping this COG in their favor was through indirect means, indicating that they sought to influence the COG through a series of objectives and efforts instead of one decisive action. Despite the offensive actions that the 3rd ACR conducted in Tal Afar to eradicate insurgent actors and support bases, they did not directly attempt to establish security by mere military presence. Rather, the unit sought to protect the people by first clearing the city of enemy fighters. The unit then shifted focus and utilized indigenous forces to hold security gains. Their intent was to prevent the reintroduction of insurgent elements into the city. Finally the 3rd ACR, Iraqi forces, and the locally elected government of Tal Afar jointly worked to build upon their successes and improve infrastructure, quality of life, and public trust in governmental capacity. Leaders in the 3rd ACR realized that these operations would not be completed rapidly. This understanding allowed them to design operations tactically to progress based on conditions, not a timetable.

The critical second step of the Tal Afar COIN campaign was formulating the tactical design of the operations. This involved boiling down the offensive, security, and reconstruction actions into manageable lines of operation, effort, and phases. The unit had no true doctrinal construct to assist them in the design and planning of their COIN operations. As a result, each of the offensive, security, and reconstruction operations were viewed as complimentary but distinct lines of effort. These three lines were the foundation for the tactical design of the unit's counterinsurgency in Tal Afar.

The "clear" line of effort (LOE) involved 3rd ACR and Iraqi forces destroying or expelling insurgent actors and foreign fighters from the city. The key tasks of this line were the implementation of population control measures (such as relocating local nationals in contentious areas of the city), establishing checkpoints, and erecting an earthen berm around the city to isolate the enemy and deny his freedom of movement.[26] Additionally, the units established a renowned detention operation that improved the security situation and provided tremendous intelligence gains.[27]

The "secure" LOE capitalized on the eradication of enemy forces during initial clearance missions and focused on the rapid enhancement of the security situation in the city. Population control measures, such as mounted and dismounted checkpoints and census data capture, were the key tasks of this line of effort. Additionally, the Iraqi army, police, and border security units were bolstered by 3rd ACR-led training programs designed to improve the capabilities of the indigenous security forces. These Iraqi forces were positioned in areas that had previously been under the control of insurgent forces, to include the territory along the Iraq-Syria border. The 3rd ACR played a decisive role in the development and oversight of these Iraqi Security Forces and were rewarded with competent Iraqi elements that extended the tactical reach of the unit.

The third line of effort was a departure from the offensive mentality that the majority of units had shared in Iraq to that point. The unit's commander, COL H.R. McMaster (a brigadier general at the time of publication), understood that it would be the "rebuilding" efforts which would allow security to endure in Tal Afar.[28] Interviews conducted with members of the unit capture the impact that this line of effort held in the tactical design:

> After the main combat operations, humanitarian and civil-affairs work quickly began in earnest. This time was crucial for maintaining trust with the local citizens and, consistent with Col. McMaster's directive to "not do the enemy's work," locals were allowed to return to their homes and were immediately offered assistance with rebuilding their neighborhoods. According to one NCO, the 3rd ACR's work included "Dropping food off, doing water drops, handing out radios to people," and a helicopter pilot noted: "Days after we went in and told the bad guys, it's time for a fight, we were there with humanitarian food, water, reparations that weren't done in Fallujah."[29]

The third and final process in designing Operation Restoring Rights dealt with refining the lines of effort to meet tactical requirements and limitations. This step

52

involved managing the tempo, transitions, and balance between the three lines of effort.

Additionally, this process allowed the unit to manage the depth and reach of its forces

and to mitigate risks to the local populace and to the security forces of both countries.

These planning factors finely tuned the design of Restoring Rights and rendered an

operation of campaign quality. The successes achieved by the 3rd ACR with respect to

tactical counterinsurgency design supports the premise that lower tactical echelons are

capable of establishing autonomous, protracted tactical COIN operations.

The 3rd ACR's successful design of Operation Restoring Rights served to thrust

McMaster's tactical approach into the global limelight. The unit's efforts throughout the

last half of 2005 were applauded by senior military leaders and politicians, including both

the Secretary of State and President George W. Bush.[30] The President, just one month

after the 3rd ACR returned from their successful tour in Tal Afar, praised the unit's

groundbreaking work in Iraq.

> [W]e changed our strategy. Instead of coming in and removing the terrorists, and
> then moving on, the Iraqi government and the coalition adopted a new approach
> called clear, hold, and build. This new approach was made possible because of the
> significant gains made in training large numbers of highly capable Iraqi security
> forces. Under this new approach, Iraqi and coalition forces would clear a city of
> the terrorists, leave well-trained Iraqi units behind to hold the city, and work with
> local leaders to build the economic and political infrastructure Iraqis need to live
> in freedom. . . . The success of Tal Afar also shows how the three elements of our
> strategy in Iraq--political, security, and economic--depend on and reinforce one
> another. By working with local leaders to address community grievances, Iraqi
> and coalition forces helped build the political support needed to make the military
> operation a success. The military success against the terrorists helped give the
> citizens of Tal Afar security, and this allowed them to vote in the elections and
> begin to rebuild their city. And the economic rebuilding that is beginning to take
> place is giving Tal Afar residents a real stake in the success of a free Iraq. And as
> all this happens, the terrorists, those who offer nothing but destruction and death,
> are becoming marginalized. . . . The strategy that worked so well in Tal Afar did
> not emerge overnight--it came only after much trial and error. It took time to
> understand and adjust to the brutality of the enemy in Iraq. Yet the strategy is

working. And we know it's working because the people of Tal Afar are showing their gratitude for the good work that Americans have given on their behalf.[31]

With this Presidential endorsement, the 3rd ACR's successful tactical COIN design had become a new standard. The Army quickly went to work to capture the lessons of Tal Afar and initial results of other tactical COIN operations in Iraq. The result was codified in FM 3-24, *Counterinsurgency*, published in December of 2006. This manual, coupled with a tactical counterinsurgency paradigm shift compelled by the 3rd ACR's success, established the groundwork for the U.S. Army's true emergence from the "Vietnam Syndrome." The Army had slowly and painfully realized that success in a COIN environment requires empowering subordinates and allowing them to leverage abilities and resources previously maintained at higher echelons of command. While the successes in Tal Afar were rendered by a brigade-equivalent organization, the idea of employing lower organizational echelons as the prime units for executing C-H-B operations began to permeate the Army.

The successes in Tal Afar sparked renewed vigor in both political and military circles and provided a promising new direction for other maligned areas of Iraq. President George W. Bush foreshadowed the wholesale implementation of similar COIN efforts in the country, particularly in the capital city of Baghdad.

> I wish I could tell you that the progress made in Tal Afar is the same in every single part of Iraq. It's not. Though most of the country has remained relatively peaceful, in some parts of Iraq the enemy is carrying out savage acts of violence, particularly in Baghdad and the surrounding areas of Baghdad. But the progress made in bringing more Iraqi security forces online is helping to bring peace and stability to Iraqi cities. The example of Tal Afar gives me confidence in our strategy, because in this city we see the outlines of the Iraq that we and the Iraqi people have been fighting for: a free and secure people who are getting back on their feet, who are participating in government and civic life, and who have become allies in the fight against the terrorists.[32]

This statement by Bush in March of 2006 set the stage for the 3rd ACR's tactical COIN design model to be utilized in the capital city. One year later the resulting operation would be dubbed the Baghdad Security Plan.

Chapter Conclusion

This chapter detailed the inception of C-H-B-like COIN operations during the Vietnam War and later in OIF. The focus of the chapter was the Army's malnourished, sickly counterinsurgency culture from 1965 to 2005 by presenting historical studies, antiquated Army doctrine, and scholarly opinions. This material created an understanding of the design challenges that 3rd Armored Cavalry Regiment faced as it designed the first successful tactical COIN operations of OIF from 2005 to 2006. We should not depart this chapter without noting that despite the achievements of 3rd ACR, no firmly established U.S. Army doctrine existed to guide them in the design of Operation Restoring Rights. Chapter 4 addresses this issue and details how several units responsible for executing COIN operations during the BSP tactically designed C-H-B operations in 2007.

---

[1]Birtle, 362.

[2]Nagl, 116.

[3]Ibid.

[4]Birtle, 363-364.

[5]Galula, 110-111.

[6]Birtle, 368.

[7]Bernard W. Rogers, *Cedar Falls-Junction City: A Turning Point* (Washington, DC: Government Printing Office, 1974), 8-12.

[8]Ibid., 15-17.

[9]Nagl, 205.

[10]Richard D. Downie, *Learning From Conflict: The U.S. Military in Vietnam, El Salvador, and the Drug War* (Westport, CT: Praeger, 1998), 109.

[11]Ibid.

[12]Ibid.

[13]Nagl, 207.

[14]Department of the Army, Field Manual (FM) 90-8, *Counterguerrilla Operations* (Washington, DC: Government Printing Office, 1986), 1-6, 1-14.

[15]Department of the Army, FM 3-24, 1-20 through 1-28.

[16]Department of the Army, FM 90-8, 1-5.

[17]Ibid., 3-2.

[18]Ibid., H-1.

[19]Galula, 110-111.

[20]Nagl, 208.

[21]Ibid., 207.

[22]David R. McCone, Wilbur J. Scott, and George R. Mastroianni, *The 3rd ACR in Tal'Afar: Challenges and Adaptations* (Carlisle, PA: Strategic Studies Institute, 2008), 5-6.

[23]Ibid., 6.

[24]Department of the Army, FM 3-24,1-6.

[25]McCone, Scott, and Mastroianni, 14.

[26]Department of the Army, FM 3-24, 5-22 through 5-23.

[27]McCone, Scott, and Mastroianni, 15.

[28]Ibid., 17-18.

[29]Ibid.

[30]The White House.

[31]Ibid.

[32]Ibid.

CHAPTER 4

TACTICAL DESIGN LESSONS FROM THE BAGHDAD SECURITY PLAN

Overview of the Baghdad Security Plan

Despite the successes earned by the 3rd ACR in Tal Afar from 2005-2006, a decidedly ominous wave of repeated violence swept the capital of Iraq in 2006. The insurgent environment had become exponentially more complex than at its start in 2003. Consisting of both disillusioned Sunni Arabs lamenting their fall from political power and politically malcontent Shiites silently supported by Iran, the insurgent movements had become malignant cancers and were moving Iraq towards civil war. The deteriorating political and military conditions forced the United States Government and Armed Forces towards a drastic change in strategy aimed at reversing this downward spiral. The change in strategy was introduced in the form of the BSP. The BSP was born out of the escalating sectarian tensions that had become catalyst to the chaotic insurgency. While much of the country was plagued by this scourge of violence, no area was as affected as the capital.

The BSP traces its origin to the ideas generated in the Ollivant and Chewning essay earlier discussed. Ollivant and Chewning presented the argument that it should be the *battalion*, not the brigade, division, or corps, which must be the prominent tactical unit of employment to reverse the worsening situation in Iraq.[1]

> The combined arms maneuver battalion, partnering with indigenous security forces and living among the population it secures, should be the basic tactical unit of counterinsurgency (COIN) warfare. Only such a battalion--a blending of infantry, armor, engineers, and other branches, each retrained and employed as needed--can integrate all arms into full-spectrum operations at the tactical level.[2]

Linda Robinson comments on their essay, successfully arguing its premise by utilizing the time-honored COIN tenets and principles of David Galula.

> The article described the varied roles such a battalion would play each day alongside Iraqi policemen and soldiers to provide security and help local officials with governing, public services, and reconstruction. It argued for placing central responsibility at the battalion level, rather than at the corps, division, or brigade, and dispersing the troops among the population rather than fortified bases away from the people and the insurgents. This dispersion scheme was drawn from the work of French counterinsurgency expert David Galula.[3]

Operational and tactical design of this "dispersion" concept presented difficulties at the start of the BSP in February of 2007. The central issue was how tactical units would plan, prepare, execute, and assess their respective actions and efforts within their own unique microcosm of insurgency. The senior tactical commander responsible for the daily execution of the BSP was Major General Joseph Fil, commander of the 1st Cavalry Division and Multi-National Division--Baghdad (MND-B). Major General Fil presented his perspective on the operational design of the BSP:

> This new plan involves three basic parts: clear, control and retain. The first objective within each of the security districts in the Iraqi capital is to clear out extremist elements neighborhood by neighborhood in an effort to protect the population. And after an area is cleared, we're moving to what we call the control operation. Together with our Iraqi counterparts, we'll maintain a full-time presence on the streets, and we'll do this by building and maintaining joint security stations throughout the city. This effort to re-establish the joint security stations is well under way. The number of stations in each district will be determined by the commanders on the ground who controls that area. An area moves into the retain phase when the Iraqi security forces are fully responsible for the day-to-day security mission. At this point, coalition forces begin to move out of the neighborhood and into locations where they can respond to requests for assistance as needed. During these three phases, efforts will be ongoing to stimulate local economies by creating employment opportunities, initiating reconstruction projects and improving the infrastructure. These efforts will be spearheaded by neighborhood advisory councils, district advisory councils and the government of Iraq.[4]

Fil's principles of "clear, control, and retain" were obviously designed as a means of approaching the counterinsurgency through the new doctrinal approach of clearing, holding, and building. The emphasis on eliminating insurgents, protecting the populace, consolidating gains, and building Iraqi capacity also shared common roots with 3rd ACR's tactical design of Operation Restoring Rights over a year prior. This statement by Fil was indicative of the U.S. Army's adoption of Galula's principles of operating at the most capable level. In the case of the BSP, it was to be at the battalion level.

Major General Fil supported Ollivant and Chewning's vision of empowering battalions as the key unit of employment within the operational design of the Baghdad Security Plan. The plan, an endeavor designed in cooperation with the Iraqi government, detailed the placement of U.S. Army battalions, Iraqi army brigades, and Iraqi police units all within the patchwork of ten security districts throughout the capital city. United States Army battalions were assigned to each of the districts and held primacy for conducting clearing operations. Holding and building operations would evolve as conditions allowed in each district, with the Iraqi forces playing more significant roles as operations and capabilities progressed. To expedite operations, a Stryker Brigade was utilized to augment the force assigned to a given area during clearance operations. This Stryker organization was serving as the operational reserve for Iraq but was allowed the flexibility to maneuver from district to district throughout execution of the BSP. This placed a greater number of clearance forces into a given security district during initial operations, all with the goal of allowing for a more rapid and successful transition to "Hold" and "Build" operations. The intent was to rapidly create a secure enough environment for the assigned forces to control the area with smaller numbers once the Stryker Brigade moved to the next district.

Photo Removed Due to Copyright Restrictions

Figure 5.   Baghdad Security Districts Drawn Under the Baghdad Security Plan
Source: The Weekly Standard (February/March 2007), 6.

The BSP was a gamble. Strategically, the United States had pinned its hope that a "surge" of five additional maneuver brigades would help to stabilize the tumultuous conditions in Baghdad. Operational risk was apparent as well. Many of the obligatory resources needed by the U.S. Army to execute the BSP were pulled from other areas of Iraq, handicapping those units' capabilities to fight the insurgency in their own operating areas. The tactical units left to execute the plan were subject to the most risk of all.

Despite being afforded significant autonomy, resources, and the underwriting of multiple layers of general officers above them, the battalions assigned to design and conduct C-H-B operations were doing so by trial and error and not by established doctrinal method. The foremost challenge for the battalions was how to implement a tactical design model for COIN that would meet the unique requirements of their specific areas of operations. While each of the battalions assigned to the security districts faced their own growing pains, perhaps none faced the daunting challenges of the units assigned to the Sadr City/Adamiyah and East Rashid Districts.

<u>Clear-Hold-Build's Formal Beginning:
The Adamiyah/Sadr City Security Districts</u>

The first battalion-level C-H-B operations of the BSP occurred in the security district of Adamiyah. These operations were led by an airborne infantry battalion from one of the five "surge" brigades to arrive for execution of the BSP. This unit was responsible for the Shiite-dominated areas of Shaab and Ur in the Adamiyah security district of northeast Baghdad. To compound the unit's already complex operating environment, the battalion was also assigned responsibility to isolate the Shiite stronghold of Sadr City. While operations inside of Sadr City were limited to select criteria because of political sensitivity, it was still a tremendously challenging area in both size and threat for a battalion to control passively.

Clearing operations began on February 14th of 2007 in Shaab. A Stryker Brigade Combat Team (SBCT) was temporarily assigned to conduct the clearance operations since the unit was capable of introducing significant manpower to the area. Zone clearance operations were conducted over the course of roughly two weeks. Strike operations, designed to target specific individuals and small groups of adversaries, were also conducted during this phase. During these two weeks, the airborne battalion responsible for the security district built combat power in the area, established outposts, and became familiar with their area of operations. As the clearance operations began to taper, the airborne battalion joined the SBCT in order to gain a first-hand understanding of the operating environment that they would soon be responsible for managing.[5]

In late February 2007, the airborne battalion took responsibility for the area and began to transition from clearance operations. The unit sub-divided Shaab and Ur into company areas of operation, where individual maneuver units would conduct smaller scale C-H-B missions. The battalion's staff conducted focused analysis and spent significant energy on developing a tactical design model which would transition the battalion into the hold and build phases. The airborne battalion faced a host of issues developing tactical COIN operations, most of which would in fact have challenged a brigade-sized organization.

First, the Shiite majority that dominated the area was almost entirely sympathetic to Jaysh al Mahdi (Army of Mahdi, hereafter, JAM), the political, military, and social organization that was aligned with the Shiite cleric Muqtada al Sadr. Muqtada al Sadr utilized Sadr City as his "capital" and fomented JAM towards violent resistance of coalition forces' presence in the area. This exacerbated the situation for the airborne battalion, basically turning all of Shaab and Ur into a giant support zone for JAM.

Secondly, the unit faced significant social and economic issues within the AO. Since Shiites were repressed so brutally and systematically by the Sunni-led government of Saddam Hussein, the preponderance of Shia peoples throughout Baghdad lived in abject poverty. They lacked consistent electricity, established sewage and water outlets, and had virtually no refuse management system.

The final major issue the battalion had to face was the state of the Iraqi Security Forces assigned to the area. The Iraqi Army units assigned to Shaab and Ur were less than 75 percent manned, while the local police were largely infiltrated by JAM. These uniformed Iraqi security forces were largely supportive of Muqtada al Sadr's directives to resist the "occupiers." The National Police unit assigned to Sadr City challenged U.S. forces was known to have active JAM leaders in its ranks, thus making the airborne battalion's task of partnering with this unit to isolate Sadr City virtually impossible.[6]

Since the tactical C-H-B operations conducted in Shaab and Ur were the first of their kind under the BSP, the battalion experienced numerous flaws in its planning and execution. First, the time-period allocated for the conduct of clearance operations was insufficient. For example, the SBCT that conducted the clearance of Shaab and Ur was allocated two weeks to complete the initial phase of the mission. Roughly 70 percent of the area within the geographical limits of Shaab and Ur was systematically cleared, but to varying degrees of thoroughness. With each of the Stryker battalions clearing an average of 675 structures per day, one has to believe that the effectiveness of the operations was marginal at best.[7] The airborne battalion discovered later that the short period allotted for initial clearance operations was woefully inadequate. As a result, the unit had to reengage its forces to clear smaller areas of terrain over the following months in order to properly clear the area.

Secondly, the airborne unit's focus was overtly enemy centric and did not embrace the Maoist and Galulan principle of securing the populace through indirect means. The overwhelming preponderance of the airborne battalion's tactical design was oriented toward neutralizing insurgence through offensive operations. The battalion had largely failed to identify the center of gravity within their COIN operations--namely winning over the people in Shaab and Ur. The unit therefore misappropriated efforts to achieve the end state and never focused on securing the "human terrain." This served to escalate tensions in the area and prevented the battalion from making measurable progress towards the goals of establishing security and civil control in Shaab and Ur.

The final, and perhaps most critical, shortcoming of the airborne battalion was its failure to establish a coherent tactical counterinsurgency design for C-H-B operations in Shaab and Ur. First, the unit never produced a definable end state. Subordinate units were torn between competing priorities: combating JAM actors, defending themselves from perceived threats, and improving security and civil stability through focus on the populace. Secondly, the airborne battalion did not establish goals and effective measures of progress. This prevented the battalion from unifying actions to achieve the desired conditions of each line of effort. Thirdly, the unit's failure to apply sound COIN methods resulted in the stagnation of progress. Had the battalion utilized a suitable tactical design methodology for COIN operations they perhaps would have established clearer priorities, goals, and unity of effort.[8] Shaab and Ur continued to be a nightmarishly complex area throughout 2007 for the airborne battalion. As a result, the Shiite insurgency that the battalion inherited in January of 2007 was still apparent after 15 months of continuous C-H-B operations. Within three months of the unit's departure, conditions demanded significant offensive operations in Ur and Sadr City. Over two hundred Shiite insurgents were killed after six weeks of combat lasting from March to May of 2008. Additionally, nearly 300 civilians were killed with another 2,100 injured during the fighting.[9] This was not what commanders had hoped for after 15 months of protracted COIN operations in the area. Had a doctrinal, tactical counterinsurgency design method existed at the time, perhaps the outcome would have been different for the airborne battalion.

Detailed analysis of the tactical design, planning, and execution of this first iteration of C-H-B operations at battalion level is key to our understanding of how the design paradigm would develop or evolve as the BSP matured. Months later, valuable lessons had been learned in subsequent C-H-B operations throughout Baghdad and a promising approach to battalion-level COIN design materialized in one of the worst regions of the capital city.

The East Rashid Security District: Formulating a Successful Battalion Level Counterinsurgency Design Model

Four months into the BSP the focus had shifted from Adamiyah and Sadr City to the opposite corner of Baghdad. The security districts of Rashid contained many of the same dynamics that existed in Shaab and Ur, but perhaps with even more complexity and intensity. Sectarian fault lines crisscrossed both East and West Rashid and turned the operating area into a patchwork of Sunni and Shiite controlled areas. One Sunni area in particular, a small community in East Rashid named Dora, had kept the attention of both operational and tactical commanders since the war's beginning four years prior.

Dora was considered the last bastion of AQIZ within the confines of Baghdad.[10] Repeated clearance operations by the infantry battalion assigned to the neighborhood created minor, temporary successes but no lasting promise of securing and stabilizing the area. It was apparent that the force allocation and tactical design of the C-H-B operations in Dora were failing midway through execution of the BSP. Operation Dragon Hammer, a focused clearance operation to disintegrate AQIZ' hold on Dora, commenced in July 2007 and continued into September. The tactical design of this three-month operation was left to the 2nd Battalion, 3rd Infantry Regiment (2-3 IN). This Stryker Infantry Battalion had operated throughout Baghdad while conducting clearance operations during each preceding phase of the BSP.

Tactically designing C-H-B operations in Dora was problematic from the start. Under the overall scheme of the BSP, senior commanders never allocated the military resources necessary to adequately clear, control, and retain Dora. At the start of the BSP, operations in the neighborhood were part of MND-B's "Supporting Effort 2" and ranked lowest on the list of priorities for resources and military forces.[11] MND-B considered Dora to be stable enough to bypass clearing and holding operations. This misperception resulted in the tasking of an inadequate force of less than a full infantry battalion to conduct operations in Dora through the spring of 2007. This small force battled insurgent forces on a daily basis, suffering what amounted to a 40 percent casualty rate.[12] The battalion in effect was unable to continue operations. The insurgency in Dora clearly had sharp teeth and required a more studied and precise approach.

As 2-3 IN began Operation Dragon Hammer, they temporarily relieved this worn-down battalion. The mission given to 2-3 IN was to root out AQIZ actors within the most contested neighborhoods of Dora, establish a secure environment, control the physical terrain, and reestablish the authority and ability of the Iraqi security forces assigned to the area. The planners for 2-3 IN worked feverishly to better understand the dynamics of the area. Before beginning operations, 2-3 IN's commanders and staff officers analyzed the

67

mission objectives listed above and established a tactical design that would guide the battalion as C-H-B operations began.[13]

The first step in 2-3 IN's tactical design of COIN operations in Dora was to identify the military objective, which fit within the larger strategic goals of the BSP. This objective was defined by a series of desired end state conditions which that were expected to exist at the conclusion of Operation Dragon Hammer. These terminal conditions were relative to security, civic infrastructure, the local economy, and capabilities of the Iraqi Security Forces.

The second step in 2-3 IN's tactical design model for Operation Dragon Hammer was to identify the core strength of the insurgent movement in Dora. However, as important as enemy considerations are in COIN operations, they understood that other things are even more critical in design. With nearly six months of C-H-B operations under their belt, 2-3 IN had realized that the crux of such operations resided in the ability to influence the populace and earn a degree of tolerance, or even acceptance of U.S. and Iraqi Forces. The battalion's tactical theme therefore became providing security to the people of Dora while returning a sense of normalcy to the community. Identification of this "tipping point" did not come easily. There was a significant insurgent density in the neighborhood and it was difficult for planners and commanders to move beyond an offensive mentality. The unit eventually realized that the strength of the enemy insurgents came from their successful intimidation campaign. It became clear that the populace of Dora could be drawn away from the insurgent cause. An offense-dominated approach, such as that used in Shaab and Ur, would not have permitted this.

The battalion next devised lines of effort to establish priorities and a rough sequencing of tactical actions. These lines of effort each contributed to the desired conditions that were to be achieved in the operations. The lines of effort devised by 2-3 IN were the following:

1. Establish a stable, secure environment

2. Build ISF capabilities

3. Restore critical infrastructure and civic capacity[14]

Each of these lines of effort was comprised of key tasks and secondary objectives that established how operations would be sequenced from one phase of C-H-B operations to the next. These tasks served as both benchmarks of progress and as tactical design guidelines.

The fourth step was the arrangement C-H-B operations in Dora. The unit realized that simply phasing operations in a linear manner would not suffice. Progress required a repeated process of analysis and assessment to determine how the various C-H-B operations would be sequenced and arranged in space and time. Certain areas of Dora presented the requisite conditions for transition earlier than others. In fact, when Operation Dragon Hammer began several pockets of terrain already possessed the conditions for the "build" phase to begin. The leadership of 2-3 IN assessed that periodic reengagement of problematic areas would preserve any initial security gains. These actions served to further strengthen the iterative approach to the battalion's tactical design.

Another aspect of establishing a depth of operations in Dora was the physical reach of the unit in the AO. Dora was significantly smaller than Shaab, Ur, and Sadr City.

The Stryker battalion was able to capitalize on this by massing forces in select, high-threat areas, while economizing elsewhere. The higher force ratio enjoyed by 2-3 IN in Dora would have perhaps improved the airborne battalion's chances of success in Adamiyah and Sadr City discussed earlier.

The final step which 2-3 IN incorporated in their tactical design model for Operation Dragon Hammer was the application of resources. This was much more involved than simply employing combat power. This involved continuous analysis and assessment to ensure that resources, predominantly in the form of Soldiers and enablers (civil affairs, explosive ordnance disposal units, psychological operations teams, technical intelligence collection assets) arrived to the right unit, at the right time, and under the right conditions. These conditions were dependent on the battalion's repeated analysis and assessments. The battalion had learned through its previous operations in support of the BSP that resource allocation was more than a simple step in the decision making process--it had to be a part of the design model for battalion level COIN operations to succeed.

Translating Operational Design to the Tactical Level

The experimental tactical COIN design model utilized by 2nd Battalion, 3rd Infantry Regiment during Operation Dragon Hammer from July to September 2007 achieved success in Dora.[15] By the end of Dragon Hammer, 15 Al Qaeda cells had been destroyed, attacks on U.S. and Iraqi troops and local civilians fell by 94 percent, Sunni sheikhs were working to improve governance and quality of life, and, perhaps most important of all from the critical perspective of the population, the Dora market had reopened. This event was monumental. It signified that the shop owners and residents of

Dora felt secure enough to return to a normal daily routine.[16]

While 2-3 IN progressed in Operation Dragon Hammer, the unit discovered that

the tactical design process they utilized was not perfect. Many of the episodic assessment

and analysis meetings ended with major alterations to key tasks and lines of effort.

Several times early in the operation, when Al Qaeda still had a stranglehold on Dora, the

tactical COIN approach was nearly abandoned for deliberate offensive operations. The

2nd Battalion, 3rd Regiment had dangerously regressed during these occasions to Mao's

counterinsurgency method of "killing the fish by polluting the water."[17] However, the

unit realized that a focused approach and a sound tactical design could produce the

terminal conditions for security to exist in Dora.

At this point, we should consider the doctrinal situation at the time of Operation

Dragon Hammer in the summer and fall of 2007. FM 3-24 had been in circulation since

December of 2006. FM 3-0 was being rewritten to incorporate the lessons and changes

from the previous six years of conflict in the GWOT. The draft of FM 3-0 current at the

time of Dragon Hammer was dated the 14th of June 2001. While this manual pre-dated

the GWOT, it still contained sound information that six years of both conventional and

counterinsurgency warfare did not negate. The most useful tool pertaining to tactical

design and planning from the 2001 edition of FM 3-0 are the elements of operational

design.

Elements of Operational Design

- End state and military conditions
- Center of gravity
- Decisive points and objectives
- Lines of operation
- Culminating point
- Operational reach, approach, and pauses
- Simultaneous and sequential operations
- Linear and nonlinear operations
- Tempo

Figure 6. Elements of Operational Design (2001)
Source: Department of the Army, Field Manual (FM) 3-0, *Operations* (Washington, DC: Government Printing Office, 2001), 5-23.

These design elements were to be used in the following regard:

> A major operation begins with a design--an idea that guides the conduct (planning, preparation, execution, and assessment) of the operation. The operational design provides a conceptual linkage of ends, ways, and means. The elements of operational design are tools to aid designing major operations. They help commanders visualize the operation and shape their intent. The elements of operational design are most useful in visualizing major operations. They help clarify and refine the vision of operational-level commanders by providing a framework to describe operations in terms of task and purpose. They help commanders understand the complex combinations of combat power involved. However, their usefulness and applicability diminishes at each lower echelon.[18]

The problem with this extract from the 2001 edition of FM 3-0 is that the complex environments found in the GWOT warranted the application of select operational level principles at the tactical level of warfare. Lower echelon units found themselves becoming reliant upon operational-level design principles for the tactical execution of COIN operations.

The planners in 2-3 IN had few doctrinal resources to aid in the development of a

suitable tactical design model for COIN. The 2001 edition of FM 3-0 provided the basic

design framework the unit utilized to developing their tactical C-H-B operations in Dora.

The importance of design of COIN operations was highlighted in the Army's new COIN

manual.

> Campaign design may very well be the most important aspect of countering an insurgency. It is certainly the area in which the commander and staff can have the most influence. Design is not a function to be accomplished, but rather a living process. It should reflect ongoing learning and adaptation and the growing appreciation counterinsurgents share for the environment and all actors within it, especially the insurgents, populace, and HN government. Though design precedes planning, it continues throughout planning, preparation, and execution. It is dynamic, even as the environment and the counterinsurgents' understanding of the environment is dynamic. The resulting growth in understanding requires integrated assessment and a rich dialog among leaders at various levels to determine the need for adaptation throughout the COIN force. Design should reflect a comprehensive approach that works across all LLOs [Logical Lines of Operation] in a manner applicable to the stage of the campaign. There should only be one campaign and therefore one design. This single campaign should bring in all players, with particular attention placed on the HN participants. Design and operations are integral to the COIN imperative to "Learn and Adapt," enabling a continuous cycle of design-learn-redesign to achieve the end state.[19]

This concept of COIN design is further elaborated upon in a subsequent paragraph

found in Chapter 4 of FM 3-24. It details the importance of constructing a viable COIN

design model:

> In *model making*, the model describes an approach to the COIN campaign, initially as a hypothesis. The model includes operational terms of reference and concepts that shape the language governing the conduct (planning, preparation, execution, and assessment) of the operation. It addresses questions like these: Will planning, preparation, execution, and assessment activities use traditional constructs like center of gravity, decisive points, and LLOs? Or are other constructs--such as leverage points, fault lines, or critical variables--more appropriate to the situation?[20]

This quote gets to the very heart of the design problem for COIN operations. It not only

acknowledges the requirement to develop a model, but poses critical questions regarding how such models must include terminology or constructs unique to counterinsurgencies and absent from operational design in major combat operations. The concept of modeling is useful in taking the broad elements of design and translating them from the operational level of war to the tactical level. The final chapters of this paper will further analyze the existing model for operational-level design and present a feasible model for designing tactical level COIN operations.

As Operation Dragon Hammer ended in September of 2005, tactical units throughout Baghdad and elsewhere in Iraq were beginning to realize the importance of sound, tactical COIN design. These formations faced numerous environmental challenges in developing sufficient models--challenges that were exacerbated by insufficient doctrine. As noted earlier, the 2001 edition of FM 3-0 only offered a rough operational-level design model. The new COIN manual, FM 3-24, was devoid of tactical design principles. Units were forced to rely upon operational warfare doctrine employed at higher levels and counterinsurgency theory (without implementing doctrine) to design their tactical operations. Such remains the case today. The U.S. Army's COIN doctrine still does not offer tactical (battalion-level and below) echelons a suitable means for designing COIN operations.

Research Questions Answered

At this point, let us revisit the research questions stated earlier in this thesis. While the following chapters serve to answer the primary research question of the paper, the first four chapters have answered each of the three secondary questions.

Secondary Question 1: Is the doctrinal guidance concerning C-H-B operations relevant and adequate to guide a battalion in designing such operations? If not, what is missing or in need of revision?

As discovered in 2007 by the battalions responsible for executing the BSP, the current approved doctrine pertaining to C-H-B operations is conceptual and not specific or methodological for units seeking to establish a sound tactical design model for COIN operations. While FM 3-24 is relevant for tactical COIN operations generally, it took application and modification of the fundamentals of operational-level design to establish a successful tactical design model for COIN operations. What proved decisive was the notion that tactical units would find the elements of operational design applicable, in contradiction to the thinking within the 2001 edition of FM 3-0. The design approach employed in Operation Dragon Hammer demonstrates that the FM 3-0 model of operational design is relevant at lower tactical echelons in a COIN environment.

Secondary Question 2: What are the common themes shared by battalions when designing successful C-H-B operations? What are the common points of failure?

This writer found the above question difficult to answer. Since lasting success in COIN operations involves extended retrospection, it is hard to ascertain common themes or elements of success. Analyzing points of failure is easier. Through analyzing C-H-B operations in Adamiyah and East Rashid it was determined that having a well-founded tactical COIN design was a deciding factor in these battalions' successes or failures. The utilization of operational-level doctrine, coupled with the conceptual framework of the C-H-B approach from FM 3-24, provided 2-3 IN with a means of developing a campaign-quality tactical design model that netted successes during Operation Dragon Hammer. As

75

of March 2009, many of the same conditions that existed at the end of Operation Dragon Hammer in September of 2007 are enjoyed by the citizens of Dora today.[21]

Secondary Question 3: Do the elements of operational design found in FM 3-0, *Operations*, adequately provide a framework for battalions to design and plan C-H-B operations successfully? If not, what is a viable structure for designing operations at the battalion level?

As outlined in the study of 2-3 IN's tactical COIN design model from Operation Dragon Hammer, the elements of operational design from the 2001 edition of FM 3-0 proved generally applicable at the battalion level--specifically in a COIN operating environment. The 2001 edition of FM 3-0 states that the "usefulness and applicability [of the elements of operational design] diminishes at each lower echelon."[22] The fact that the success of the BSP hinged on the ability of individual battalions to design autonomous and protracted COIN operations contradicts this statement. From what has been determined thus far, perhaps the following statement should be added: "However, in counterinsurgency operations, this usefulness and applicability of operational design increases at lower echelons because of the nature of the operations themselves."

While the elements of operational design, coupled with COIN theory from FM 3-24, served to guide 2-3 IN's tactical design for C-H-B operations in Dora, doctrinal improvements must be made. Specifically, a more precise and standardized model addressing how lower tactical echelons should design COIN operations is absolutely necessary in order for the positive lessons learned from this operation to benefit other engaged units across the Army. Chapter 5 of this paper addresses this requirement by integrating the Army's newest evolution of operational design found in the 2008 edition

of FM 3-0 with tactical COIN lessons from OIF.

Chapter Conclusion

The cases studies presented in this chapter support the central premise that

battalions are the prime unit of employment in C-H-B COIN operations, as previously

discussed in the essay of Ollivant and Chewning. These case studies have allowed each

of the three secondary research questions to be answered. The following chapter

addresses the paradigms of operational design and presents tactical modeling

considerations for battalions faced with designing C-H-B operations.

---

[1]Ollivant and Chewning, 50-51.

[2]Ibid.

[3]Robinson, 121.

[4]Major General Joseph Fil Jr., Commanding General Multi-National Division, Baghdad and 1st Cavalry Division, Press Conference, (February 16, 2007, 9:05 a.m. EST).

[5]Robinson, 127-129.

[6]Supported by materials from the After Action Report (AAR) of 2nd Battalion, 3rd Infantry Regiment, Baghdad, Iraq, February, 2007.

[7]Ibid.

[8]Ibid.

[9]Sholnn Freeman and Ernesto Londono, *The Washington Post*, May 11, 2008. http://www.washingtonpost.com/wp-dyn/content/article/2008/05/10/ AR2008051000626.html (accessed February 16, 2009).

[10]Robinson, 309.

[11]Multi-National Division-Baghdad, "Breaking the Cycle of Sectarian Violence: Security Operations in Baghdad," Information Paper, Headquarters, Multi-National Division-Baghdad, 2006.

[12]Supported by materials from the After Action Report (AAR) of 2nd Battalion, 3rd Infantry Regiment, Baghdad, Iraq, September 2007.

[13]Ibid.

[14]Ibid.

[15]Robinson, 309-311.

[16]Ibid.

[17]Russell F. Weigley, *The American Way of War: A History of the United States Military Strategy and Policy* (Bloomington, IN: Indiana University Press, 1973), xxii.

[18]Department of the Army, FM 3-0, 5-23, 5-24.

[19]Department of the Army, FM 3-24, 4-9.

[20]Ibid., 4-3.

[21]Based on March 2009 discussions between the author and operational planners serving in MNC-I Headquarters.

[22]Department of the Army, FM 3-0, 5-23, 5-24.

CHAPTER 5

DEVELOPING A TACTICAL DESIGN MODEL

Reevaluating Tactical Design of
Clear-Hold-Build Operations in 2008

The earlier analysis of the methodical development of tactical C-H-B operations from the Vietnam War to the BSP has rendered two results. First, the contemporary Army has come recently to embrace Galula's precept that achieving success in COIN requires the lowest tactical echelons to work with the greatest autonomy.

> The subdivision should be carried out down to the level of the basic unit of counterinsurgency warfare: the largest unit whose leader is in direct and continuous contact with the population. This is the most important unit in counterinsurgency operations, the level where most of the practical problems arise, and in each case where the war is won or lost.[1]

In the case of U.S. Army COIN operations since the beginning of the GWOT, this unit was specifically demonstrated as the maneuver battalion.

Second, for over four decades no doctrine has been created to address how tactical formations should design COIN operations. From 1965 to 2005, the Army largely fought insurgencies at the operational and strategic levels. The successes of 3rd ACR in Tal Afar from 2005 to 2006 (as well as the general failure of conventional threat-based tactics) forced the Army to reevaluate the level at which defeating insurgent movements most effectively occurs. While COIN is a political movement in the end, the Army should best serve the strategic end state by allowing lower tactical formations to wage protracted, individualized campaigns against the specific dynamics of insurgency in compartmented areas. To enable tactical echelons to accomplish their own COIN objectives in support of the broader military end state, it is critical that a feasible tactical design model be created to guide the development of future battalion-level C-H-B operations.

In February of 2008, the newest version of FM 3-0, *Operations*, was released. This edition provides roughly the same conceptual model for operational design as its predecessor from 2001, with the subtle difference that it does not rule out the application of operational design principles at the tactical level.

> *Operational design* is the conception and construction of the framework that underpins a campaign or major operation plan and its subsequent execution. . . . This operational design provides a framework that relates tactical tasks to the strategic end state. It provides a unifying purpose and focus to all operations. . . . These are tools to help clarify and refine their concept of operations by providing a framework to describe its execution. They help commanders understand, visualize, and describe complex combinations of combat power and help them formulate their intent and guidance. The elements of operational design may be used selectively in any operation. . . . They help refine and focus the concept of operations that forms the basis for developing a detailed plan or order. During execution, commanders and staffs consider the design elements as they assess the situation. . . . Commanders and staffs gauge how the elements of operational design relate to the mission variables. The applicability of individual elements varies with echelon. Generally, all apply at the strategic and operational levels. Some have no tactical relevance whatsoever. . . . Ultimately, commanders at each echelon determine which elements are relevant, based on the mission and conditions.[2]

The conditions which warrant C-H-B missions support the premise that most of the elements of operational design are indeed relevant at the tactical level. The purpose of this chapter is to analyze the operational design model presented in the 2008 edition of FM 3-0 to determine how to best translate it to a tactical-level model for COIN operations. The resulting product should answer the primary research question of this paper.

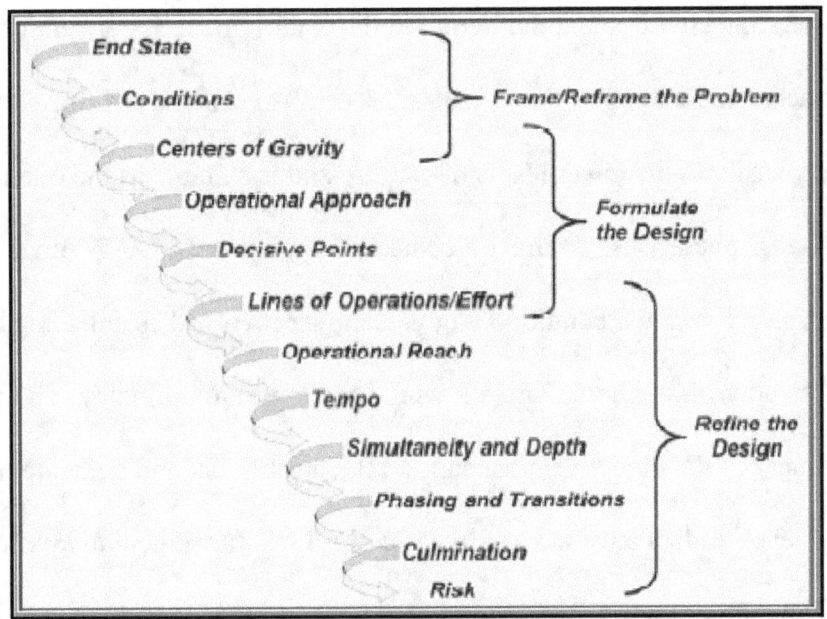

Figure 7.   Elements of Operational Design (2008)
Source: Department of the Army, Field Manual (FM) 3-0, *Operations* (Washington, DC: Government Printing Office, 2008), 6-7.

Defining End States

As the airborne battalion tasked to conduct C-H-B operations in Adamiyah could attest, a clearly defined end state is essential to COIN operations. An end state guides unity of effort, facilitates integration and synchronization, and aids in reducing risk during each phase of C-H-B operations.[3] Echelons at the operational level of war guide efforts towards reaching the strategic end state. However, tactical echelons remain focused on achieving a military end state. This lower echelon military end state is best termed the "Tactical Counterinsurgency Objective." In military context an "objective" is a clearly defined and achievable element that all efforts should be directed towards.[4] In OIF during 2007 the operational-level military end state derived from the OIF Joint Campaign Plan was the creation of "a stable Iraq, under the rule of law, maintaining civil order, and denying safe haven for extremists."[5] Generally this end state would work in

81

any COIN operating environment that required the commitment of conventional forces and the protracted application of the C-H-B approach. An end state of this nature translates very easily to the lower levels of warfare and is suitable as the overall objective for tactical C-H-B operations. To illustrate this point, the tactical COIN objective identified by 2-3 IN during Operation Dragon Hammer involved establishing continued security and stability throughout Dora allowing for a return to normalcy. Though this localized, tactical COIN objective must support the operational and strategic military end state, tactical level leaders must never forget that COIN is fundamentally political in nature. While battalion-level C-H-B operations should retain focus on the tactical COIN objective, the political element must at least be considered.

> the political power is the undisputed boss. . . . What is at stake is the country's political regime, and to defend it is a political affair. Even if this requires military action, the action is constantly directed toward a political goal. Essential though it is, the military action is secondary to the political one, its primary purpose being to afford the political power enough freedom to work safely with the population.[6]

One cannot lose sight of this fundamental principle of COIN.

Establishing Terminal Conditions

Although not yet publicly released, FM 3-24.2, *Tactics in Counterinsurgency*, offers a fine example of the general terminal conditions for tactical C-H-B operations. These conditions are identified as the key prerequisites of the tactical COIN objective or military end state.

	Functioning legitimate government that does not require external support
Safe, secure and stable environment established	
Rule of Law established	Essential services restored
	Economic foundation with sufficient infrastructure established
Self Sufficient National Security Forces Established	Increased support to the HN Government

Figure 8.   C-H-B Terminal Conditions

Source: Department of the Army, Field Manual (FM) 3-22.4 (Draft), *Tactics in Counterinsurgency* (Washington, DC: Government Printing Office, 2008), 4-6.

Each of these conditions represents the goal of a particular line of effort. As COIN efforts begin to achieve defined progress these goals become more capable of being realized. When all of these enabling conditions are achievable, so is the tactical counterinsurgency objective.

Centers of Gravity

Dr. Jack Kem states that "there is no COG at the tactical level but decisive points instead."[7] The 2008 edition of FM 3-0 offers the same argument, but replaces "decisive points" with "objective."[8] Dr. Kem's argument provides the more ideal construct for tactical COIN operations with one caveat: there is only one decisive point in a tactical C-H-B campaign and that is "Winning the People."

While this decisive point appears to be anecdotal, we have already seen from our examination of counterinsurgency literature how important is this idea of operating to win the populace. David Kilcullen presents the following regarding this notion:

> control over the population is the goal [of] both the government and the insurgent--but the enemy and the terrain still matter. Terrain-centric and enemy-centric actions are still vital and crucial to success as the enemy and terrain still matter, but the population is the key to successful COIN operations.[9]

Perhaps the best concise statement is Galula's premise that "the people are the prize."[10]

The counterinsurgent's idealist goal of "winning the people" is difficult to accomplish, hence its decisive nature. The surest means to successfully achieving this decisive point is by securing the environment. It is additionally necessary to win the peoples' tolerance and support, even if merely passive in nature. Successful information engagements in each phase of tactical operations, and within each line of effort, serve as the critical enabler for achieving this decisive point. Winning the support of the people is largely a function of perception management. Therefore, information operations are critical functions of a counterinsurgent forces tactical design. To illustrate the singular importance of winning the people, below is an extract from the 2007 OIF Joint Campaign Plan indicating the operational COG:

> The Center of Gravity is the broad support of the Iraqi people for the Government of Iraq. Support of the people will have a positive effect on security and provide a solid foundation for reconciliation. Furthermore, broad support of the government by the people of Iraq will help ensure the Coalition support necessary to see the campaign to completion.[11]

The operational COG supports both the military and political conditions that are to exist at end state. The concept of "winning the people" as the tactical decisive point provides the same impetus as the operational COG, but does so in a practical and succinct way that translates very well at the battalion level.

84

Operational Approach

Operational approach, by definition, is the manner in which a unit contends with a center of gravity.[12] Operations may be designed utilizing the direct approach, meaning that effects and goals are achieved by the application of resources and forces directly oriented towards the center of gravity. Since "winning the populace" represents the decisive point that allows tactical C-H-B operations to reach the counterinsurgency objective, it is only feasible that an indirect operational approach should be utilized. The indirect approach incorporates incremental means to securing gains along each line of effort in order to reach an overall tipping point where conditions will allow the force to achieve the tactical objective. This is a stark reminder of the failed COIN efforts from the Vietnam War. Tactical units attempted to kill their way out of an insurgency in Southeast Asia and never embraced the indirect approach of gradually "winning the hearts and minds."

Winning the people is a process that involves persistence and repetition of action. It involves trial and error, reengagement, and negotiating success through non-military means (such as contracting local help to restore essential services or using emergency response funding to stimulate a neighborhood's economy). Each of these factors represents indirect means to an end state. It also involves the willingness to default to non-lethal means--an aspect of COIN which our modern Army is slow to embrace and that the Vietnam-era Army failed to court altogether.

Cause and effect also plays a tremendous role in achieving progress. Emplacing a sewer system to improve sanitation and quality of life may seem like a direct means to progress. What happens though when the lead contractor is found to be a part of the insurgent support base and has been overcharging in order to siphon funds into the enemy's coffers? This type of complex or poorly structured problem permeates many aspects of a counterinsurgency. Designing and planning operations within a C-H-B framework must involve analysis of cause and effect and means to measure the effects. It also lends further support to Nagl's theory that the indirect approach is the only feasible method to winning a COIN campaign since problems of this nature are typically solved by systematic approaches and not by some singular action.

Outlining Decisive Points

Decisive points, in the context of operational design, are physical, measurable, or assessable tasks and objectives that indicate progression towards achieving desired effects and the overall end state. In the context of tactical C-H-B operations, this operational-level definition is best represented by the term "Key Tasks." Key tasks are identified as critical steps of progression towards reaching the decisive point and facilitating the enabling conditions to achieve the tactical counterinsurgency objective. Keys tasks are collated into respective lines of effort and should be arranged in logical sequence. It is important that units do not utilize the arrangement of these key tasks as a checklist for progress, but rather as an "azimuth" for progression towards achieving the terminal conditions of each line of effort because many of the key tasks may be more complex than originally thought.

Building Sound Lines of Effort

Field Manual 3-0 states that the operational-level design fundamental of identifying decisive points "shape[s] the design of operations. They help commanders select clearly decisive, attainable objectives that directly contribute to establishing the end state."[13] In order to shape the design of tactical C-H-B operations, these decisive points (identified as key tasks at the tactical level) are grouped into categories by effort. These efforts are thematic and are utilized to focus resources and effects. The November 2007 draft of FM 3-24.2, *Tactics in Counterinsurgency*, offers a viable solution for grouping key tactical tasks into broader lines of effort. This example serves as a highly feasible model for battalions to utilize for establishing key tasks and lines of effort.

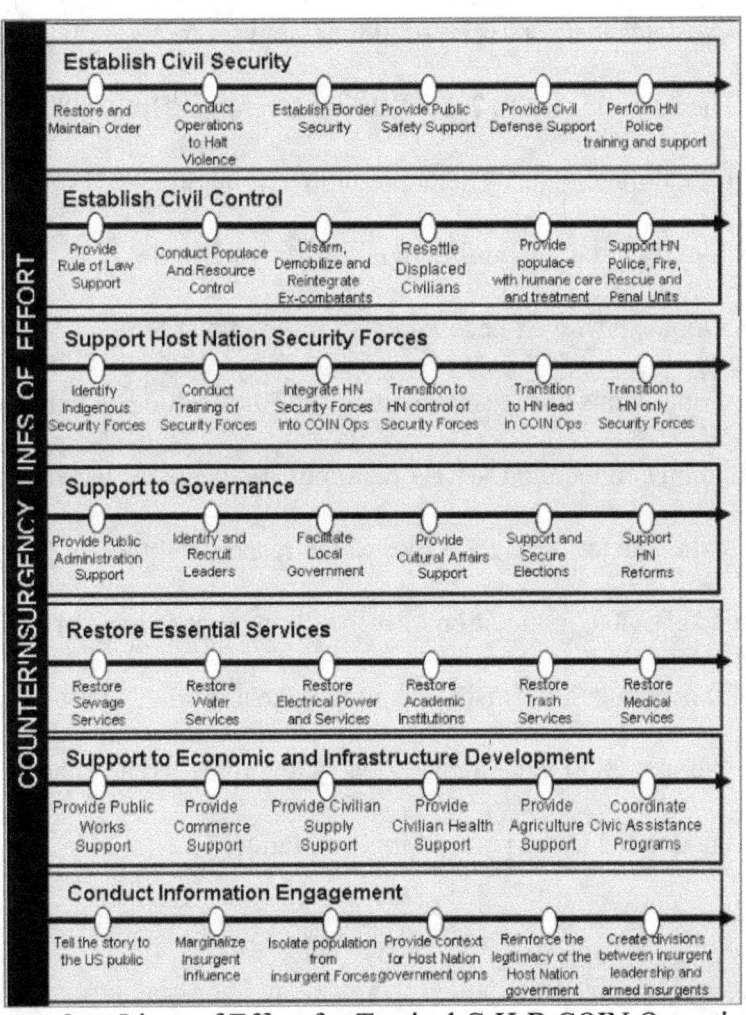

Figure 9.   Lines of Effort for Tactical C-H-B COIN Operations
Source: Department of the Army, Field Manual (FM) 3-24.2 (Draft), *Tactics in Counterinsurgency* (Washington, DC: Government Printing Office, 2008), 4-6.

87

Operational Reach

This first step in the "refine" phase of the operational design model from FM 3-0 is interesting. "Reach" in the context of operational design involves both the physical distance and duration that a force can extend its full capabilities through the area of operations.[14] Tactical units should be keen to consider the effects that COIN operations have on friendly forces and available resources. For instance, establishing the boundaries of an area of operations requires analysis of force ratios between insurgents, counterinsurgents, and inhabitants vying for room to operate within the given terrain. Field Manual 3-24 states that for every 1000 inhabitants a force of 20-25 Soldiers should be allocated.[15] The AO assigned to 2-3 IN during Operation Dragon Hammer had approximately 19,000 inhabitants. The unit employed roughly 400 U.S. Soldiers in Dora. The doctrinal ration required the minimum allocation of 240 Soldiers. The enemy situation in Dora alone, however, necessitated a more robust force package and a narrowed area of operations to focus the capabilities of the 400 Soldiers. Comparatively, the airborne battalion conducting C-H-B operations in Shaab, Ur faced an impossible ratio, especially when factoring in their overwatch responsibilities for Sadr City. A full one-fifth of Baghdad's 2007 population of 6.1 million persons resided in the Shaab-Ur-Sadr City area. This population density meant that the airborne battalion faced a ratio of roughly one Soldier per 2800 inhabitants. Clearly, the force's reach had been dramatically overextended to the point of mission failure.

Other factors beside force allocation are critical when considering the extent of a unit's tactical reach. Basing, sustainment facilities, and non-standard enablers (such as persistent cameras and monitoring devices) serve to extend aspects of a force's tactical reach. Interagency support, military and police training teams, and joint force enablers (such as aerial reconnaissance and collection platforms or electronic warfare capabilities) also improve a tactical unit's ability to extend itself in an area of operations. These capabilities also improve the endurance of a unit and the consequent tactical campaign capability.[16] Without this ability to maintain protracted operations, the resolve and persistence required to meet the target conditions of each line of effort would go unfulfilled in most situations. This aspect of reach is a critical component of each line of effort. If the local people do not believe that the military force has the "staying power" to achieve the target conditions, the populace will most likely tend to favor the cause of the insurgent.

The last aspect of tactical reach is understanding culmination in COIN operations. Culmination stems from a lack of manpower, inadequate resources and enablers, or the inability to establish security objectives within an AO, or a combination of each. Had the airborne battalion in Adamiyah not received augmentation from other units in the summer of 2007, their operations may have culminated by the fall of that year. It is crucial for units to know or anticipate where these culmination points exist in time and physical space. The examination of culmination points is an independent step in the FM 3-0 operational level design model. Lower echelon units should consider it in conjunction with their analysis of tactical reach since culmination correlates directly to the other elements of tactical reach.

Managing Tempo

This next step in operational design offers the greatest contrast between major combat operations and COIN operations at tactical level. "Tempo", defined by FM 3-0, is "the relative speed and rhythm of military operations over time with respect to the enemy."[17] At the operational level of war, analyzing tempo is an independent step in the design process. At the tactical level, specifically in a COIN operating environment, tempo management encompasses the next two steps of the operational model as well: simultaneity and depth, and phasing and transition.

Tempo management in tactical C-H-B operations is difficult. The principal focus of this step is to design operations to allow for the ability to rapidly respond to critical events. This ability must be carefully balanced with patience to preserve endurance as well as tactical reach.

Tempo management includes the fundamental operational design step of "simultaneity and depth" by arranging various clear, hold, and build operations throughout space and time. As learned by 3rd ACR in Tal Afar, C-H-B operations are designed as sequential, complimentary operations that require repetitive application. To illustrate this point, the airborne battalion that conducted C-H-B operations in Shaab and Ur benefited from having a Stryker brigade conduct a majority of the initial clearance operations. As noted earlier, the two weeks allocated to clear their assigned AO were insufficient and that subsequent, multiple clearance operations had to be executed in order to adequately transition to hold and build operations throughout much of their AO. In this case, "tempo" was adversely affected by the inability of the battalion to diversify efforts through the depth of their area. Instead, the airborne battalion had to concentrate its resources on conducting focused operations within a narrowed area in order to properly manage the tempo and progression of operations into the hold and build phases.

Establishing criteria for transitions between the various phases and themes in tactical COIN operations could provide the basis for a thesis of its own. In the context of establishing a tactical design model for C-H-B operations, "phasing and transitioning" equates to establishing measures of effectiveness along each line of effort. These measures serve to indicate when the requisite conditions exist for operations to transition from one tactical theme to the next (such as when operations shift from clear to hold to build). It is important to note that "transition" does not always equate to "progress." The example above regarding the airborne battalion conducting C-H-B operations in Adamiyah clearly indicates that the unit had to reengage select areas--a tactical regression that was required in order to eventually move forward with hold and build operations. Again, the iterative nature of the COIN operating environment may warrant taking small steps backward to make progressive strides forward.

Risks Inherent with Clear-Hold-Build Operations

Managing risk is one of the more difficult tasks during tactical design of C-H-B operations. The paradox of COIN operations is "the more you protect the force, the less secure you make it."[18] This premise alludes to the fact that success in COIN operations means that the force is outside of its safe areas and operating amongst the populace--the same terrain in which the enemy is working. It is crucial that units accept risk; sometimes to include high risk at critical points in time and space during COIN operations. The tactical counterinsurgency objective in Dora during Operation Dragon Hammer necessitated considerable risk to the forces conducting clearing and holding operations. While risking the protection of the individual Soldier was a conscious decision by commanders on the ground, this risk was made palatable by the realization that minimized troop risk equated to higher risk of mission failure.

Risk management is an implied facet of design and planning in all Army operations. It would therefore be easy to omit it as a step in the tactical C-H-B design process. In the COIN operating environment, however, balancing risk and reward is a key component in planning operations. Perhaps the reach of a unit is restricted because the force ratio is inadequate. In this case, a battalion commander may choose to spread his forces throughout the AO in smaller units (such as platoon combat outposts) to expand his reach. This naturally introduces more risk into the operation because it removes the ability to mass Soldiers and resources in a timely manner. This conscious assumption of increased tactical risk may be warranted because the commander believes it mitigates overall risk to the mission. If a particular neighborhood of the AO were to be reengaged and cleared of threats that may have returned following initial clearance operations, the commander may choose to shorten his tactical reach and provide a higher force ratio for the operation. This tethering would mitigate risk for the Soldiers themselves. Because risk management is so integrated with other tactical design aspects, it must remain as an independent and conscious step within the design process for tactical COIN operations.

Chapter Conclusion

The synthesis of battalion-level COIN operations executed during the BSP along with current Army doctrinal principles has yielded what may be considered the rudiments of a suitable tactical COIN design model. The fact that neither FM 3-24 nor FM 3-22.4 presents a model for designing such operations has already been discussed in detail earlier. The final chapter of this paper addresses this doctrinal shortcoming and offers a design model for tactical echelons to utilize in the development of C-H-B COIN

operations.

---

[1]Galula, 110-111.

[2]Department of the Army, FM 3-0, 6-25 to 6-28.

[3]Ibid., 6-32.

[4]Ibid., A-1.

[5]Multi-National Force--Iraq, "Update to Joint Campaign Plan: Operation Iraqi Freedom" (Baghdad, Iraq: Headquarters, MNF-I, November 27, 2007).

[6]Galula, 89.

[7]Jack D. Kem, *Campaign Planning: Tools of the Trade,* 2nd ed. (Fort Leavenworth, KS: U.S. Army Command and General Staff College, 2006), 45.

[8]Department of the Army, FM 3-0, 6-8.

[9]David Kilcullen, "Counterinsurgency in Iraq: Theory and Practice" (Quantico, VA: Small Wars Center of Excellence, September 26, 2007).

[10]Galula, 7-8.

[11]Multi-National Force--Iraq.

[12]Department of the Army, FM 3-0, 6-9.

[13]Ibid., 6-12.

[14]Ibid., 6-15.

[15]Department of the Army, FM 3-24, 1-13.

[16]Department of the Army, FM 3-0, 6-15.

[17]Ibid., 6-16.

[18]Department of the Army, FM 3-24, 1-27.

CHAPTER 6

CONCLUSIONS AND RECOMMENDATIONS

Research Conclusions

The study of United States Army COIN efforts and doctrine from Vietnam through our current conflict in Operation Iraqi Freedom has yielded several key conclusions. First, the U.S. Army of today has pushed COIN warfare to the lowest, feasible tactical levels--a practice not evident in Vietnam or at the start of Operation Iraqi Freedom. The design of the Baghdad Security Plan, utilizing battalions as the units of employment to conduct protracted, autonomous COIN operations, clearly illustrates this change in thinking.

Second, the nature of modern operations designed around modular Brigade Combat Teams indicates that the practice of decentralizing COIN operations in future conflicts will likely continue. Battalion-level tables of organization and equipment have benefited from the modularized force structure. Further improvements, resulting largely from the lessons provided from continued conflict, will make the maneuver battalion an even more capable and robust organization, preserving and enhancing its ability to design, plan, and conduct independent C-H-B operations.

The third and final conclusion drawn from research stems from the previous two. Considerations for designing and conducting tactical COIN operations must take a different tack. If a corporal fighting at the tactical level can impact the strategic environment, then is it really a stretch to think that our modern tactical formations, particularly maneuver battalions, should require operational-level planning and design tools in a COIN environment? The answer is clearly no. Battalions currently committed

94

to fighting the insurgent movements in both Iraq and Afghanistan are largely operating in the operational sphere of warfare and will continue to do so. History has proven that strategic counterinsurgency outcomes are intimately connected with the tactical environment. Therefore, as our war-fighting doctrine continues to evolve it must address this paradigm shift.

Each of these conclusions is drawn from the vast amount of historical literature and contemporary theory on combating insurgent movements. Theorists such as Galula, Krepinevich, and Kilcullen have all shaped the current standard of how best to employ conventional military formations to defeat an asymmetric threat. The brilliance of Ollivant and Chewning in recognizing the need for a shift in COIN methodologies provided the impetus for what may eventually be regarded as the intellectual turning point for Coalition success in Iraq. Their work also provided the traction necessary for the Army as an institution to improve, learn from successes and failures, and employ combat formations and tactical design theory effectively in COIN operations.

A Tactical Design Model for Battalion Level Clear-Hold-Build Operations

The primary outcome of this paper is that the operational design model found in the 2008 edition of FM 3-0, with relevant perspective refinements, works at the tactical level. Today's operating environment has grown to such levels of complexity that tactical formations are required to design, plan, implement, and execute COIN operations which are largely of campaign quality. Such was the case for the airborne battalion in Adamiyah and 2nd Battalion, 3rd Infantry in Dora during Operation Dragon Hammer. Both of these battalions were given the autonomy to conduct protracted, tactical COIN operations--

95

fifteen months, as was the case for the airborne battalion in Adamiyah. Such levels of commitment require addressing the problem and the means to solving it beyond the tactical level. Thus battalions, which in recent years have undergone significant growth in capabilities, must look beyond the tactical level of counterinsurgency and work to design and meet operational military objectives.

The elements of operational design from FM 3-0 can be re-tooled to meet the needs of battalion-level formations as they develop tactical solutions to counter insurgent movements. This reworked tactical design model is presented below.

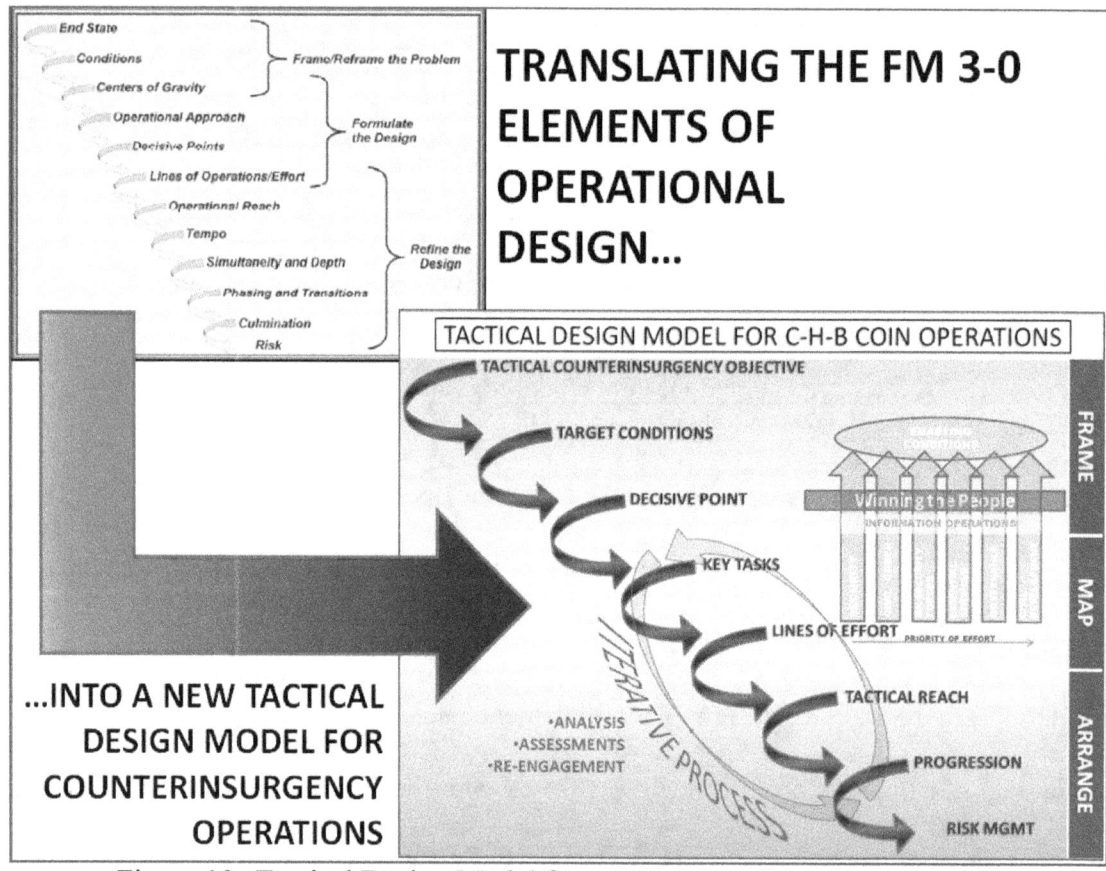

Figure 10. Tactical Design Model for a C-H-B Operating Environment
Source: Author's design (using Department of the Army, Field Manual (FM) 3-0, *Operations* (Washington, DC: Government Printing Office, 2008), 6-7).

This model is presented as a feasible, doctrinally sound, and historically

supported solution to altering operational-level design principles to correspond with

tactical counterinsurgency operations. Operational level "End State" is replaced with

"Tactical Counterinsurgency Objective" which, when achieved, contributes to meeting

the operational military end state. "Target Conditions" represent the states that must exist

within each line of effort in order for the tactical COIN objective to be achieved. The

operational concept of "Center of Gravity" does not exist at the tactical level. Rather, a

"Decisive Point," a tipping point of success, exists. In the case of tactical C-H-B

operations, this decisive point is winning over the populace to support the security,

stability, and reconstructions efforts of the counterinsurgent force and host nation

government. These three steps in the model are the critical guideposts that drive tactical

COIN design. Failure to properly frame or define these steps results in a fundamentally

flawed endeavor from the onset. Therefore, it is inherent that critical thought be applied

to frame the tactical design during these first three steps. For this reason, the portion of

the model is shaded red to indicate the importance of analyzing and identifying the

integral factors that the rest of the tactical design hinges upon.

The second stage of tactical design involves mapping the key tasks that must be

fulfilled in order to create the target conditions and achieve the tactical objective. These

key tasks must be grouped and organized within lines of effort. The lines should be

ordered as logically as possible to provide some context for analyzing progression. The

six lines of effort depicted in the model represent the COIN lines of effort identified in

FM 3-24: Security, Civil Order, Host Nation Security Force Development, Restoration of

Essential Services, Support to Governance, and Civil Development. The study of classical COIN operations identifies these lines as key components for defeating an insurgent movement. "Conducting Information Operations" is omitted because it is an enabling function, not a distinct line of effort. Information operations contribute to progress in each line of effort and are vital in achieving the decisive point of "Winning the People." The logical ordering of key tasks within a respective line of effort is important because it allows commanders to prioritize and visualize future operations. This stage of the model is shaded amber because of the representative problems that may be introduced to the design of tactical COIN operations if the key tasks and corresponding lines of effort are not identified, arranged, and prioritized correctly.

The final stage of tactical design, labeled "Arrange," is shaded green because the inclusive steps are the enabling components for planners to facilitate success. The first step in this stage is to understand and to incorporate tactical reach into C-H-B operations. The notion of reach involves applying resources, managing force ratios to meet mission requirements, and understanding how and where culmination may exist within the design framework. The step labeled "Progression" refers to metrics. Commanders and planners always seek to identify the measures of success or failure to gauge the efficacy of COIN operations. This step of the design process establishes the measures of performance and effectiveness. These indicate when clearing operations can transition to holding operations and when holding operations can advance to building. Conversely, identification of the failure to progress serves to indicate when reengagement must occur to solidify the conditions for continued progress. This step, as do each of the rest of the steps in the "Arrange" and "Map" stages, relies upon iterative analysis, assessment, and reengagement to eventually reach the decisive point of winning the people, fulfilling the

98

target conditions for success, and achieving the tactical counterinsurgency objective. Lastly, the risk management process is applied as a litmus test. This is to ensure that the arrangement of C-H-B operations within the design framework is suitable for accomplishing the tactical COIN objective and for protecting the force and the populace. This process is listed as separate step, despite being an intuitive process in all military operations, because the commander is responsible for continuously assessing, assuming, and mitigating the various and potentially catastrophic risks that exist in a COIN operating environment.

This model answers the primary research question and attempts to present a suitable design model for the development of protracted tactical COIN operations utilizing the C-H-B approach. While this model is not universal, in the sense that it may not work for all units or in all situations, it is born from the theory and practice of tactical COIN operations over the past six decades spanning numerous conflicts, doctrinal frameworks, and operating environments. The United States Army has drawn upon these historical lessons during its overhaul of war-fighting doctrine throughout the past several years. The doctrine which emerged has shown significant recent maturation in U.S. COIN theory. Hopefully the current U.S. Army COIN doctrine will continue to be improved as the experiences and lessons learned by combat forces in the current counterinsurgencies are captured. The model found in Appendix A could be a worthwhile addition to the next evolution of tactical COIN doctrine.

Recommendations

Despite the recentness of FM 3-24, the U.S. Army's COIN doctrine development is anything but stagnant. The creation of the joint U.S. Army and U.S. Marine Corps

99

Counterinsurgency Center in 2006 preserved the momentum of developing the practices and theory required to counter modern insurgent movements.

While FM 3-24 provides the theory for contemporary COIN operations, the concepts it presents are of a higher order. As indicated throughout this thesis, the manual does not provide concrete tools for tactical level commanders, staff officers, and leaders to utilize for the development and execution of tactical COIN operations. Such was the case when the BSP began in February 2007. FM 3-24 was less than three months old at the time and offered very little in the way of design elements to tactical units and leaders. Commanders were forced to adopt ad hoc counterinsurgency practices to meet the demands of their respective areas of operation when C-H-B operations began in February 2007. For this reason, it is important that the development and indoctrination of tactical-level COIN methodologies be institutionalized for future use.

The most salient recommendation stemming from this research is for the U.S. Army to adopt the tactical design model presented in this paper and incorporate it in FM 3-24.2, *Tactics in Counterinsurgency*, before its official release. This model would be a firm addition to Chapter 4 of the manual, entitled "Comprehensive Tactical Planning in Counterinsurgency." Section two of the chapter, labeled "Tactical Design in Counterinsurgency," seems ideally suited to present such a model but one does not exist in the manual's November 2007 draft. The only design tool found in Chapter 4, section two of the manual is an in-depth presentation of how the common COIN lines of effort should be incorporated in tactical COIN operations. Adding the results of this research would serve to improve FM 3-24.2 by providing units with a means for designing protracted, tactical counterinsurgency operations.

Continued Study

The U.S. Army as an institution would benefit from the continued research and study of the applicability of campaign design and planning fundamentals within tactical echelons. While most operational themes are best left to joint, operational-level campaign design parameters, there are many merits to the notion that tactical formations are capable and better suited for establishing campaign-type frameworks in protracted COIN operations. Current doctrine and force structure have already placed the Brigade Combat Team at the heart of the Army's war-fighting capabilities. Perhaps it is time to allow these organizations the resources and latitude to develop subordinate campaign-quality enduring operations in irregular warfare operating environments.

Throughout the development of this paper, materials from the National Defense University's Institute for National Strategic Studies and Center for Technology and National Security Policy provided broader conceptual understanding for the development of U.S. COIN doctrine. Many resources exist in digital format and may be accessed at http://www.ndu.edu/research.cfm.

Any attempt to grasp the fundamentals of tactical COIN design would be wasted without first understanding insurgent and counterinsurgent theory. Reading Galula's *Counterinsurgency Warfare: Theory and Practice* is essential. The fact that the development team for FM 3-24 utilized it as a *primary* reference is indicative of the book's importance. It still holds as much relevance today as when Galula penned it forty-five years ago.

Those readers with access to secure internet protocol networks would benefit from studying the classified after action reports of 3rd Armored Cavalry Regiment's lessons in Tal Afar from 2005-2006. Likewise, 4th Brigade, 1st Infantry Division, 2nd Brigade, 82nd Airborne Division, and 3rd Brigade, 2nd Infantry Division (SBCT) all published classified after action reports at the conclusion of their combat tours operating in support of the BSP. These AARs are valuable tools to understand the complexity of tactical C-H-B operations and the necessity for sound tactical COIN design fundamentals.

These reports, along with the experiences harvested from other brigades and battalions who executed tactical COIN operations in Iraq and Afghanistan since 2007, will contribute to the next evolution of doctrine. Hopefully the U.S. Army will accept the "new" paradigm of counterinsurgency as a form of warfare that it will be required to execute in foreseeable conflict, and will act to prevent these particular lessons of the Global War on Terror from becoming the subject of institutional amnesia. There has been far too much invested in blood and treasure, and too much at stake nationally and internationally, to continue suffering from the Vietnam syndrome of American defeat in counterinsurgency operations.

GLOSSARY

Al Qaeda. Sunni terrorist organization that fuels the Global War on Terror. Elements of this group are responsible for acts of terrorism, fomenting insurgency, and inciting sectarian violence within Iraq. The term used to describe Al Qaeda (AQ) actors and their efforts in the country of Iraq is AQIZ. Alternate spellings for Al Qaeda are al-Qaida or al-Qa'ida.

Battalion. Basic unit assigned to design and execute COIN operations in independent areas of operation. The term "battalion" should be considered as a generic label in the context of this paper. It is used to represent echelon of command and organizational structure and not a specific Infantry, Stryker, or Combined Arms unit as found in current modular BCT organizational designs.

Brigade Combat Team. The United States Army unit responsible for physically executing the preponderance of tactical level actions.

Baghdad Security Plan. The campaign in the capital of Iraq that began with the "surge" of U.S. forces (5 additional BCTs) and was designed to reduce violence and destabilization in the Iraqi capital. The plan involved dividing the capital city into ten security districts and then allocating U.S. and Iraqi forces to each zone with the intent of re-establishing order and diminishing terrorist, insurgent, and sectarian violence. This campaign lasted from February to November of 2007 and was often referred to by its Arabic name "Fardh al Qanoon" roughly translating to "Imposing the Law."

Clear-Hold-Build. A doctrinal approach to COIN operations involving three discrete, generally consecutive phases: *clearing* a selected area of insurgent actors, *holding* the terrain against future insurgent buildup, and *building* popular support, infrastructure, and resistance to future insurgent activity in the area. This COIN approach is outlined in the December 2006 edition of Field Manual 3-24, *Counterinsurgency*.

Coalition Provisional Authority. The interim, U.S.-led transitional government that filled the executive, legislative, and judicial voids once the Iraqi government was dissolved in April 2003. This authority terminated in June of 2004 once the interim Iraqi Government was appointed.

Combined Action. An alternative approach to COIN operations. This approach involves embedding U.S. forces in host nation formations to conduct COIN efforts. This type of approach only works in environments where the threat and efficacy of insurgent forces is minimal.

Counterinsurgency. An environment where dissent of selected groups or actors is directed toward a governing body or actions of a government.

Full Spectrum Operations. The operational concept outlined in FM 3-0 (2008) that details the simultaneous application of offensive, defensive, stability, and civil support operations to achieve desired and proportional results.

Host Nation. The nation in which a military operation is conducted.

Limited Support. An approach to COIN involving limited, direct military action. The purpose of Limited Support is to advise and develop the capacity of host nations to execute their own COIN operations. Foreign Internal Defense (FID) is a classic example of this COIN approach.

Line of Effort. A line that links multiple tasks and missions using the logic of purpose--cause and effect--to focus efforts toward establishing operational and strategic conditions.

National Reconciliation. A movement sparked by coalition forces in Iraq to help the Iraqi government reestablish validity and strength. Also viewed as a movement to unify the efforts of the various religious sects and governmental entities against the spread of Islamic extremism and the movements of Al Qaeda in Iraq.

Operational Design. The conception and construction of the framework that underpins a campaign or major operation plan and its subsequent execution. It provides a unifying purpose and focus to all operations (FM 3-0, 2008, 6-6). This concept does not indicate design at the operational level of war, but rather a construct for designing operations regardless of level.

Operating Environment. The phrase use to characterize the conditions that exist on a battlefield or in an area of operation.

The Surge. Colloquialism for influx of U.S. military forces into Iraq during the 2007-2008 timeframe. "The Surge" was the enabling condition that allowed for the execution of the Baghdad Security Plan. It included five U.S. Army Brigade Combat Teams and two U.S. Marine battalions. While "The Surge" and the "Baghdad Security Plan" are not necessarily synonymous, they were indeed symbiotic.

APPENDIX A

TACTICAL DESIGN MODEL FOR C-H-B COIN OPERATIONS

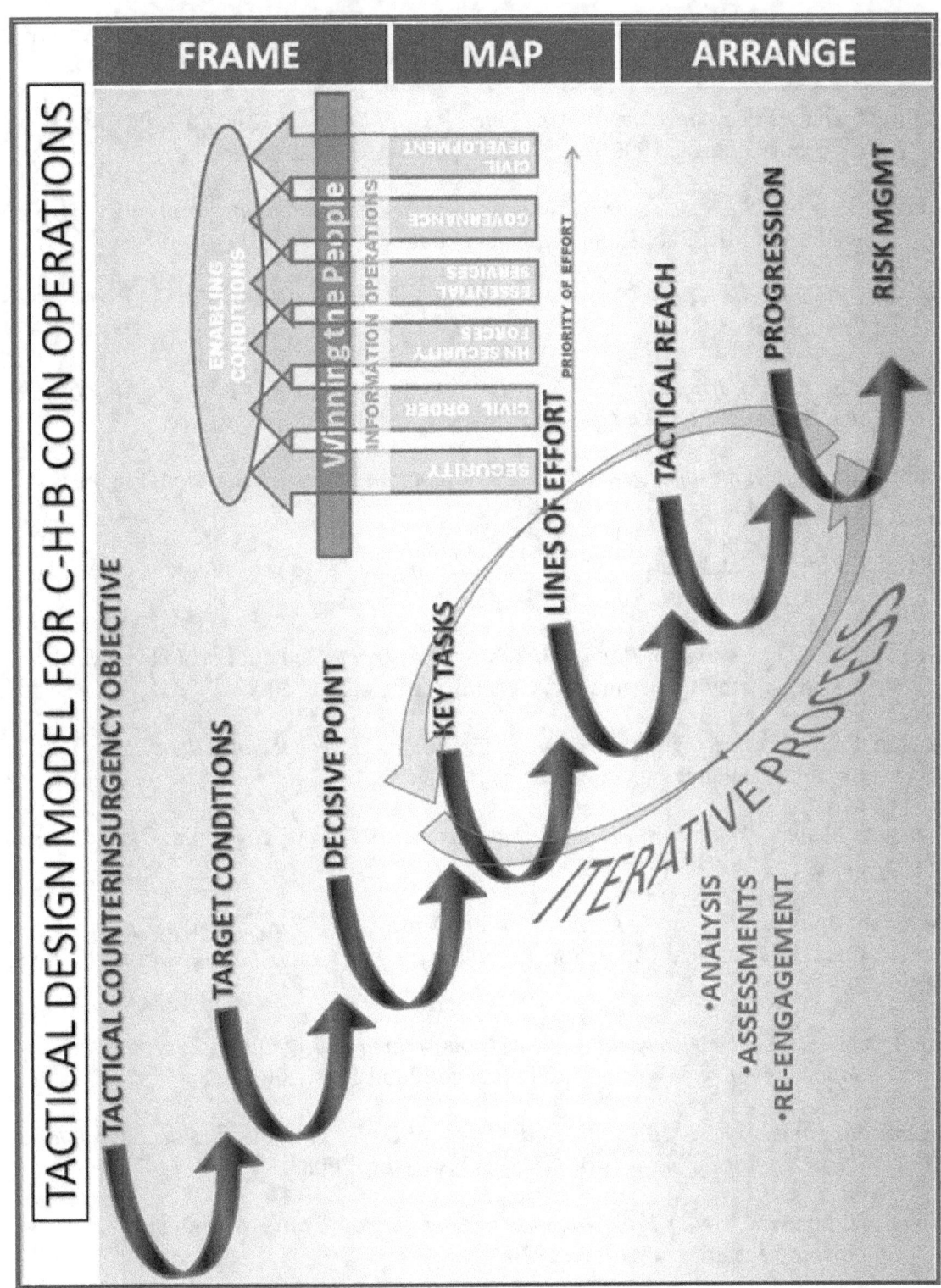

105

BIBLIOGRAPHY

Books

Birtle, Andrew J. *U.S. Army Counterinsurgency and Contingency Operations Doctrine: 1942-1976.* Washington, DC: Center for Military History, 2006.

Calwell, Charles E. *Small Wars: Their Principles and Practice.* Lincoln, NE: Univeristy of Nebraska Press, 1996.

Corum, James S. *Bad Strategies: How Major Powers Fail in Counterinsurgency.* St. Paul, MN: MBI Publishing Company, 2008.

———. *Fighting the War on Terror : A Counterinsurgency Strategy.* St. Paul, MN: Zenith Press, 2007.

Downie, Richard D. *Learning From Conflict: The U.S. Military in Vietnam, El Salvador, and the Drug War.* Westport, CT: Praeger, 1998.

Galula, David. *Counterinsurgency Warfare: Theory and Practice.* London, England: Praeger, 1964.

Gardner, Lloyd C., and Marilyn B. Young. *Iraq and the Lessons of Vietnam.* New York, NY: The New Press, 2007.

Kem, Jack D. Dr. *Campaign Planning: Tools of the Trade.* 2nd ed. Fort Leavenworth, KS: U.S. Army Command and General Staff College, 2006.

Kitson, Frank. *Low Intensity Operations: Subversion, Insurgency and Peacekeeping.* London, England: Faber and Faber, 1971.

Marston, Daniel. *Counterinsurgency In Modern Warfare.* New York, NY: Oxford Press, 2008.

McGrath, John J. *Boots on the Ground: Troop Density in Contingency Operations.* GWOT Occasional Paper, Fort Leavenworth, KS: Combat Studies Institute Press, 2006.

Nagl, John A. *Counterinsurgency Lessons from Malaya and Vietnam: Learning to Eat Soup with a Knife.* Westport, CT: Praeger Publishers, 2002.

Robinson, Linda. *Tell Me How This Ends: General David Petraeus and the Search for a Way Out of Iraq.* New York, NY: PublicAffairs, 2008.

Rogers, Bernard W. *Cedar Falls-Junction City: A Turning Point.* Washington, DC: Government Printing Office, 1974.

Weigley, Russell F. *The American Way of War: A History of the United States Military Strategy and Policy*. Bloomington, IN: Indiana University Press, 1973.

West, Francis J. *The Strongest Tribe : War, Politics, and the Endgame in Iraq*. New York, NY: Random House, 2008.

Woodward, Bob. *The War Within: A Secret White House History 2006-2008*. New York, NY: Simon and Schuster, 2008.

Periodicals and Articles

Gomport, David C., and John Gordon. *War by Other Means: Building Complete and Balanced Capabilities for Counterinsurgency*. Santa Monica, CA: Rand, 2008.

Kagan, Kimberly. *Enforcing the Law: The Baghdad Security Plan Begins*. Washington, DC: The Institute for the Study of War, 2007.

———. *From 'New Way Forward' to New Commander*. Washington, DC: The Institute for the Study of War, 2007.

Kilcullen, David. "Counterinsurgency in Iraq: Theory and Practice." Quantico, VA: Small Wars Center of Excellence, September 26, 2007.

———. Field Notes Compiled in Baghdad, Taji, and Kuwait City. "Twenty-Eight Articles: Fundamentals of Company-Level Counterinsurgency." March 29, 2006.

Komer, Robert W. *Bureaucracy Does its Thing:Institutional Constraints on U.S.-GVN Performance in Vietnam*. Santa Monica, CA: Rand, 1972.

Krepinevich, Andrew F. Jr. "How to Win in Iraq." *Foreign Affairs* 84, no. 5 (September/October 2005): 87-104.

Petraeus, David H. "Learning Counterinsurgency: Observations from Soldiering in Iraq." *Military Review* (January/February 2006): 2-12.

Pirnie, Bruce, and Edward O'Connell. *Counterinsurgency in Iraq, 2003-2006*. Santa Monica, CA: Rand, 2008.

Serwer, Daniel, and Sam Parker. *Iraq After the Surge: Options and Questions*. Washington, DC: United States Institute of Peace, 2008.

Research Papers

Ahern, Colin. *Clear, Hold, Build: Modern Political Techniques in COIN.* Scholarly Paper, Fort Campbell, KY: 2008.

Burgess, Kenneth J. "Organizing for Irregular Warfare: Implications for the Brigade Combat Team." Thesis, Naval Postgraduate School, 2007.

Davis, Sean P. "Making the Spoon: Analyzing and Employing Stability Power in Counterinsurgency Operations." Monograph, School of Advanced Military Studies, Command and General Staff College, 2007.

DeTreux, Kenneth M. "Contemporary Counterinsurgency (COIN) Insights from the French-Algerian War (1954-1962)." Strategy Research Project, Army War College, 2008.

Evans, Michael R. "Clear, Hold, and Build: The Role of Culture in the Creation of Local Security Forces." Monograph, School of Advanced Military Studies, Command and General Staff College, 2006.

Graff, Jonathan K. Jr. "United States Counterinsurgency Doctrine." Thesis, Command and General Staff College, 2004.

Gubler, Justin C. "Reconciling Counterinsurgency with Civil War: A Strategy for Stabilizing Iraq." Strategy Research Project, Army War College, 2007.

Higgins, James M. "The Misapplication of the Malayan Counterinsurgency Model to the Strategic Hamlet Program." Thesis, Command and General Staff College, 2001.

McCone, David R., Wilbur J. Scott, and George R. Mastroianni. "The 3rd ACR in Tal'Afar: Challenges and Adaptations." Professional Paper, Strategic Studies Institute, 2008.

Metz, Steven, and Raymond Millen. "Insurgency and Counterinsurgency in the 21st Century: Reconceptualizing Threat and Response." Scholarly Essay, Strategic Studies Institute, 2004.

Miller, Thomas Erik. *"Counterinsurgency and Operational Art: Is the Joint Campaign Planning Model Adequate?"* Monograph, School of Advanced Military Studies, Command and General Staff College, 2003.

Ollivant, Douglas A., and Eric D. Chewning. "Producing Victory: Rethinking Conventional Forces in Counterinsurgency Operations." *Military Review* (July-August 2006): 50-59.

Wipfli, Ralph, and Steven Metz. "Coin of the Realm: U.S. Counterinsurgency Strategy." Research Project, Carlisle Barracks, PA, January 10, 2008.

Government Documents

Department of the Army. Field Manual (FM) 3-0, *Operations*. Washington, DC: Government Printing Office, 2001.

———. Field Manual (FM) 3-0, *Operations*. Washington, DC: Government Printing Office, 2008.

———. Field Manual (FM) 3-07, *Stability Operations*. Washington, DC: Government Printing Office, 2008.

———. Field Manual (FM) 3-24, *Counterinsurgency*. Washington, DC: Government Printing Office, 2006.

———. Field Manual (FM) 3-24.2, *Tactics in Counterinsurgency* (Draft). Washington, DC: Government Printing Office, November 17, 2008.

———. Field Manual (FM) 90-8, *Counterguerrilla Operations*. Washington, DC: Government Printing Office, 1986.

Department of the Navy. *Small Wars Manual*. Washington, DC: Government Printing Office, 1987.

Multi-National Division--Baghdad. "Breaking the Cycle of Sectarian Violence: Security Operations in Baghdad." Information Paper, Headquarters, Multi-National Division--Baghdad, 2006.

Multi-National Force--Iraq. "Joint Campaign Plan: Operation Iraqi Freedom." Baghdad, Iraq: Headquarters, MNF-I, November 27, 2007.

Petraeus, David H. General. "Multi-National Force--Iraq Commander's Counterinsurgency Guidance." Baghdad, Iraq: Multinational Forces-Iraq, June 21, 2008.

Simmering, Michael J., Major. After Action Report, *Final Report of 3d Armored Cavalry Regiment Operations in Operation Iraqi Freedom, Period Covered 06 MAR 05-21 FEB 06*. Fort Carson, CO: 3rd Armored Cavalry Regiment Headquarters, 2006.

US Army Battle Command Training Program. "4-3 Brigade Combat Team COIN Seminar," 22-25 January 2007. Fort Leavenworth: BCTP, January 22, 2007.

Other Sources

Fil Jr., Major General Joseph, Commanding General Multi-National Division, Baghdad and 1st Cavalry Division. Press Conference, February 16, 2007, 9:05 a.m. EST.

Freeman, Sholnn, and Ernesto Londono. *The Washington Post.* May 11, 2008. http://www.washingtonpost.com/wp-dyn/content/article/2008/05/10/ AR2008051000626.html (accessed February 16, 2009).

Rice, Condoleezza. Press Conference, October 19, 2005. http://www.state.gov/secretary/ rm/2005/55303.htm (accessed September 20, 2008).

The White House. News Release, March 20, 2006. http://www.whitehouse.gov/news/ releases/2006/03/20060320-7.html (accessed December 6, 2008).